# THE AGE OF
# DINOSAURS

**Jane Burton** trained as an artist and illustrated many natural history books with drawings before turning to photography. Her main books of photographs include *Animals of the African Year, Small Animals, The Colourful World of Animals* and, more recently, *The Book of the Year* and *Nightwatch*.

**Dougal Dixon** has been fascinated by dinosaurs and other extinct life forms from an early age. He studied geology and palaeontology at the University of St Andrews, and he is now a writer and editor of earth science subjects. His book *After Man – A Zoology of the Future* has been published in twelve languages.

# THE AGE OF
# DINOSAURS
# A PHOTOGRAPHIC RECORD

## JANE BURTON
## Text by DOUGAL DIXON

SPHERE BOOKS LIMITED
London and Sydney

First published in Great Britain by Sphere Books
Ltd 1984
30–32 Gray's Inn Road, London WC1X 8JL

ISBN 0 7221 2108 3 (paperback)
ISBN 0 7221 2109 1 (hardback)

TRADE
MARK

Set in Times New Roman

**Authors' acknowledgements**

Jane Burton acknowledges her debt to Bruce
Coleman, who once casually remarked, 'Have you
thought about photographing dinosaurs?'; to Kim
Taylor, for his invaluable technical advice and
continual encouragement; to Jan Taylor, for taking
photographs for use as backgrounds; to Weycolour
Ltd, Godalming, for the care and speed with which
they processed the film; and to Nick Eddison and
Ian Jackson, who kept the whole project running
smoothly.

Dougal Dixon joins Jane in extending a warm note
of appreciation to Steve Kirk, the artist whose skill
and hard work has enabled the animals to be so
realistically shown in photographic form.

**This book was produced in association
with Bruce Coleman Limited**

AN EDDISON · SADD EDITION

Edited, designed and produced by
Eddison/Sadd Editions Limited
2 Kendall Place, London W1H 3AH

Phototypeset by Tradespools Limited,
Frome, Somerset, England
Origination by Reprocolor Llovet S.A.,
Barcelona, Spain
Printed and bound in Hong Kong by
Mandarin Offset International Limited

# CONTENTS

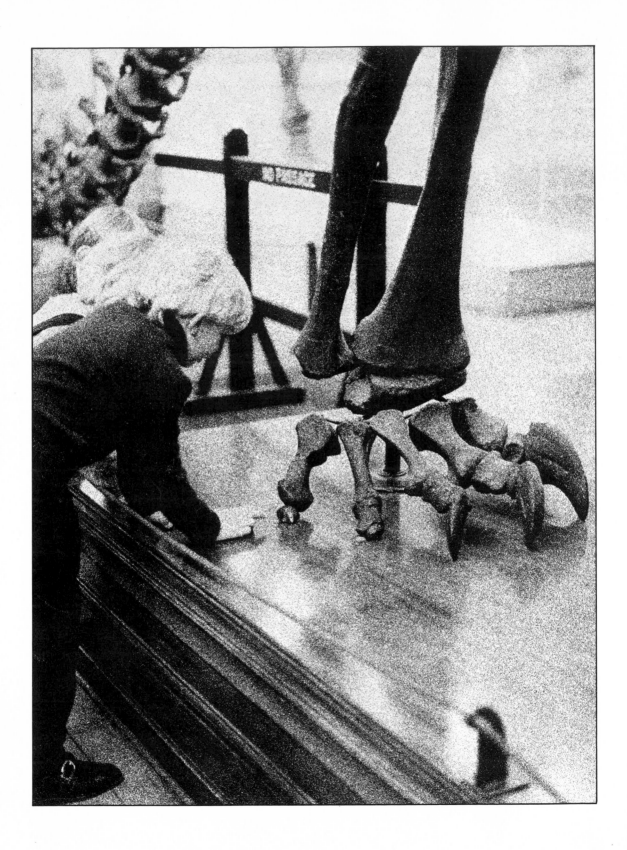

# INTRODUCTION

There are few among us who have not looked at a dinosaur skeleton and wondered what the real animal must have been like in life, what sort of country it lived in and the kinds of sounds it made. Many of us have imagined ourselves back in the ancient past, in the jungles stalking huge creatures that no-one else has ever seen. Or our imaginations have brought these animals to our time and we have visualized them beside well-known landmarks in our cities. The skeletons of the dinosaurs and the other great animals of the past are magnificent enough mounted in museums, but they can hardly convey the grandeur of such animals in real life. Paintings of the creatures abound. But paintings are still paintings, however well executed, and few artists can capture the drama and atmosphere of a time long lost. Artwork alone cannot portray these long-dead animals as dynamic, vigorous living creatures. Photographs can, however. The photographs in this book are mainly of the dinosaurs themselves, but also of many of the other fascinating reptiles of the past.

In the introductory pages we learn how palaeontologists – scientists who study fossil life forms – have come to know many thousands of types of extinct animals. Undoubtedly millions more wait to be discovered. Yet it is the dinosaurs among these known types that excite the greatest wonder and fascination. But it is important to remember that the term 'dinosaur' is not a scientifically recognized classification. In popular use it should only be applied to members of two orders, the Saurischia and Ornithischia. Often the term is misused and applied to pterosaurs, ichthyosaurs, plesiosaurs, and even mammals.

In the main part of the book – the photographic section – we shall see the first reptile, scurrying lizard-like among the ferns of the coal forest. From this we can watch the reptile line diverting into its main branches; one branch into early dominance with the development of the mammal-like reptiles; another into aquatic crocodile-like forms. Later we can observe how the roles of these two groups are then reversed, the mammal-like reptiles becoming small and insignificant mammals, and the crocodile-like forms expanding into the dinosaurs that were to rule the Earth for 120 million years. The book finishes with the end of the Age of Dinosaurs and the passing of the great reptiles of the time. Since then, 65 million years ago, the mammals have grown to dominance and the reptiles have dwindled into insignificance.

The world will never see the likes of the great reptiles again. We feel the loss at never having seen them in real life. However, now we can observe them through the lens of the camera, and we can travel backwards in time to observe these one-time masters of the world while they were at the peak of their success.

Museum skeletons still continue to excite our curiosity but they cannot show us what the giant reptiles really looked like, or how they lived.

# THE CHANGING EARTH

The hills and mountains of our planet seem to have stood immobile since time began and will stand till the crack of doom. Yet the hills are not very old, compared with the 4,600 million year age of the Earth; and the higher, more impressive the hills, the younger they are. The magnificent Himalaya range of mountains on the border of Tibet are a mere 50 million years old – just youngsters in the geological timescale.

Not only mountains, but all the physical features of the world, can be thought of as rather short-term structures. Rivers, lakes, uplands, downlands, forests, deserts, even the positions of the continents; they have all changed, and are continuing to change daily.

How do we know? We know because the lost landscapes have left their evidence, as clear as the image on a photographic film. The next time you take a walk in a rocky area, have a close look at the rocks. The ground on which you are treading may once have been below the sea, and if that is the case there will be some evidence for it. The rock may be chalk, made from limy mud deposited in shallow water, or it may be sandstone, formed from heaps of sand washed down from a river. There may be fossils of seashells in it. The shells may be of animals that are totally extinct now, or they may be of animals still living today. If they are of present-day animals they may be of a type that is only found in another part of the world, giving evidence for the great change of climate as well as of geography.

It is possible, on the other hand, that the rocks are volcanic in origin, formed from cooled lava flows that are proof of a violent youth, so different from the

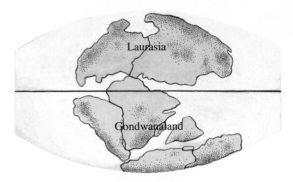

The continents are always moving. 180 million years ago, at the height of the Age of Dinosaurs, they were all joined together in two great landmasses (*above*). In the north was Laurasia, and in the south was Gondwanaland.

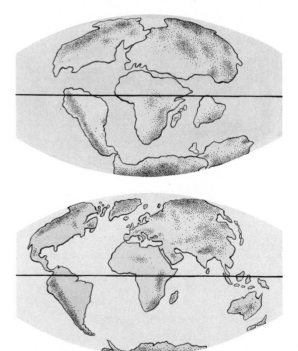

During the Age of Dinosaurs the continents began to split up and drift apart (*centre*) until they reached the positions they are in today (*above*). They are still moving – at a rate of centimetres per year.

serene, untroubled landscape of today. Or they may be rocks that have been baked and twisted by incredibly strong pressures, trapped in the roots of a mountain range as it was thrust upwards, the mountains themselves being later worn down to their bases.

The continents are vast rafts of rock, drifting here and there, driven by the movements of the Earth's mantle deep below the crust. 180 million years ago North America was joined to Europe. Since then North America has been drifting westwards, crumpling up its western coastline as it goes and forming the mountains now found there. The Himalayas have been built by the sub-continent of India colliding with the rest of Asia and crushing up rocks and sediments.

We can work out the movements of continents by examining the magnetism in their rocks. When a rock forms, any magnetic particles in it align themselves with the Earth's north and south poles. These particles are then fixed and remain in this position wherever the rock goes, just as the magnetic particles are aligned on a video tape at the time of recording. Nowadays we can examine these magnetic particles, find out which direction they point in, and work out where the rock must have been when they were first aligned.

The study of these ancient landscapes is known as palaeogeography. Through studying the rocks we can work out the landforms and scenery of times past. We can tell whether a particular extinct animal lived in swamps, by the seashore, in upland valleys, in mountains, or wherever, just by the kind of rock in which its remains were found.

Not only were the continents in different positions in times past, but the coastlines and the positions of mountains and inland seas on those continents were quite different. This map shows the coastline of present-day North America superimposed on that of Jurassic North America. The inland sea separated western mountains from eastern plains.

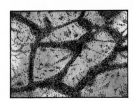

Ancient landscapes and climate conditions are often recorded in the rocks. Current bedding (*top*) was formed by a river, mud cracks (*left*) by drying waterholes, and ripple marks (*right*) by wave action in shallow sea.

# PLANT LIFE ON THE EARTH

When we think of fossils we usually think of the fossils of animals. Plants, however, also become fossilized, and the study of fossilized plants, palaeobotany, is very important in helping us visualize ancient landscapes and environments.

Plants are known as 'primary producers' – they make their own food from water and minerals in the soil, using the energy of sunlight. This food is used by them, and also by the animals that eat them. Herbivorous animals may in turn be eaten by carnivorous ones. The plants, then, provide the first link in a food chain, and the type of animals present in an area depends on the type of plants that grow there.

Fossils of one of the earliest groups of land plants come from Devonian rocks in the north of Scotland. These knee-high psilophytes were very primitive, with no proper leaves or flowers. They clothed the banks of a great inland lake in a region of mountains and deserts.

Grasslands, for example, give rise to grazing animals.

Different types of vegetation are found in different parts of the world, depending on the geography and climate. Different types of vegetation are found throughout time as well, as one plant type evolved from another. At first, all plants were single cells and lived in the sea. The one cell carried out all the living functions, from feeding to reproduction. Later, multi-celled seaweeds evolved from them. In these the different cells had different functions. Leaf cells generated the food, stem cells anchored the plant, reproductive cells were responsible for reproduction, and so on. Eventually, some of the plants that were washed ashore were able to survive on damp land. They developed supportive structures to keep them upright, and a plumbing system to carry water from the soil up to the leaves, and food from the leaves down to the rest of the plant.

The character of the plant life of the Earth has changed through time. Ferns (1) evolved 350 million years ago and have changed very little since then. Grass (2), on the other hand, is a newcomer, only appearing about 50 million years ago. *Cooksonia* (3) was one of the first plants to come out on to land about 400 million years ago, but there is nothing like it about today. The humble horsetails (4) are as old as the ferns; small forms can still be found but at one time they grew into great trees.

Great forests then developed. But the plants of these forests were primitive by today's standards. They consisted of early relatives of the ferns and horsetails, but growing to heights of 30 metres (100 feet) or more. When they died, the forests became buried in the mud of the swamps in which they grew and eventually their wood turned into coal.

Later these primitive forests gave way to coniferous trees, and finally to flowering plants with their complicated reproductive structures. So the vegetation became similar to that of today.

This changing plant pattern preceded the changing animal pattern. At first there was no oxygen in the atmosphere. Oxygen only built up as it was given off by the plants as a by-product of the food-making process. Once the plants were out of the water and on land, then the animals were able to leave the sea as well. As each type of plant came and died out, then the particular animals that fed on it came and died out with them. The early ferns were eaten by the mammal-like reptiles. The later coniferous trees were browsed by the dinosaurs. When, eventually, grasses evolved a mere 50 million years ago grazing animals, like the antelope, evolved to feed on them.

# ANIMAL LIFE ON THE EARTH

Like plants, animals started small. Single-celled animals moved about in the ancient oceans, living by swallowing up the single-celled plants. From such beginnings they evolved into many-celled animals, some of which later developed backbones. Some of the vertebrates came out of the water, developing successively into amphibians, reptiles and mammals.

It is the different stages in this process that we use when we are determining geological time. The geological timescale is split up into a number of periods, each period indicating some stage of animal evolution.

Very few fossils are found from the Precambrian period, before 570 million years ago. This is because during these early times animals had no hard parts, such as bones or shells, that would fossilize easily. The Cambrian period is marked by the sudden development of hard anatomy, and hence a sudden increase in fossils.

In the Ordovician the first jawless fishes developed and in the Silurian period their numbers increased greatly. In Devonian times animal life moved out on to land, which the plants had recently colonized in the Silurian. Insects and spiders were first, but they were followed later by the fishes, which developed into amphibians. The first vertebrates to leave the water were freshwater fishes, stranded when their lakes dried out. By developing lungs and

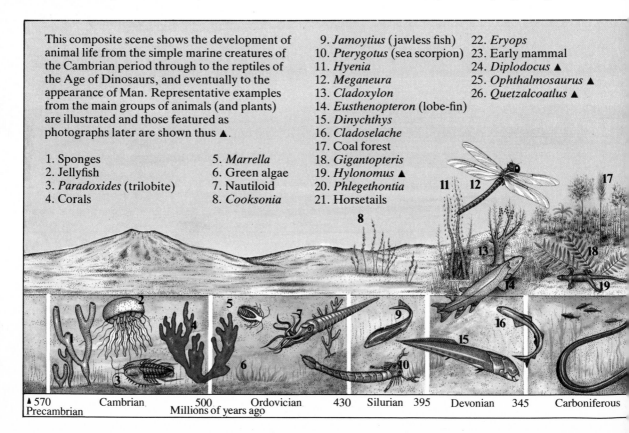

This composite scene shows the development of animal life from the simple marine creatures of the Cambrian period through to the reptiles of the Age of Dinosaurs, and eventually to the appearance of Man. Representative examples from the main groups of animals (and plants) are illustrated and those featured as photographs later are shown thus ▲.

1. Sponges
2. Jellyfish
3. *Paradoxides* (trilobite)
4. Corals
5. *Marrella*
6. Green algae
7. Nautiloid
8. *Cooksonia*
9. *Jamoytius* (jawless fish)
10. *Pterygotus* (sea scorpion)
11. *Hyenia*
12. *Meganeura*
13. *Cladoxylon*
14. *Eusthenopteron* (lobe-fin)
15. *Dinychthys*
16. *Cladoselache*
17. Coal forest
18. *Gigantopteris*
19. *Hylonomus* ▲
20. *Phlegethontia*
21. Horsetails
22. *Eryops*
23. Early mammal
24. *Diplodocus* ▲
25. *Ophthalmosaurus* ▲
26. *Quetzalcoatlus* ▲

▲ 570 Precambrian · Cambrian · 500 · Ordovician · 430 · Silurian · 395 · Devonian · 345 · Carboniferous

Millions of years ago

paired muscular fins they were able to struggle across land to reach the next pool of water.

During the Carboniferous period the amphibians were the rulers of the coal forests. It was at this time that the first reptile appeared, laying its tough-shelled egg which gave protection to its young.

The reptiles became very successful on land during the Permian period which followed. One group of reptiles adopted some very mammal-like characteristics.

Later, in the Triassic, the mammal-like reptiles began to die out, eventually becoming extinct, but not before they gave rise to the mammals themselves. The early mammals were small, shrew-like creatures, changing very little in appearance for the next 130 million years. They were in the background of evolutionary development all this time because the dinosaurs came to dominance in the Triassic, and remained dominant through the Jurassic and Cretaceous periods. These three periods, the Triassic, Jurassic and Cretaceous, are known as the Age of the Dinosaurs.

At the end of the Cretaceous, some 65 million years ago, all the dinosaurs died out, and the Age of Mammals began. The Age of Man did not arrive until the advent of the Quaternary period, a mere 2 million years ago.

Nearly all the divisions in the geological timescale are based on the changes in sea animal life, since the rocks of the various ages are usually represented by marine deposits. The names of the periods are mainly derived from the places in which the particular rocks were first studied. Devonian rocks are typical of the type found in Devon in southern England, for example. The Carboniferous takes its name from the carbon of the coal, but in the United States of America geologists subdivide this period into Mississippian and Pennsylvanian, after those areas.

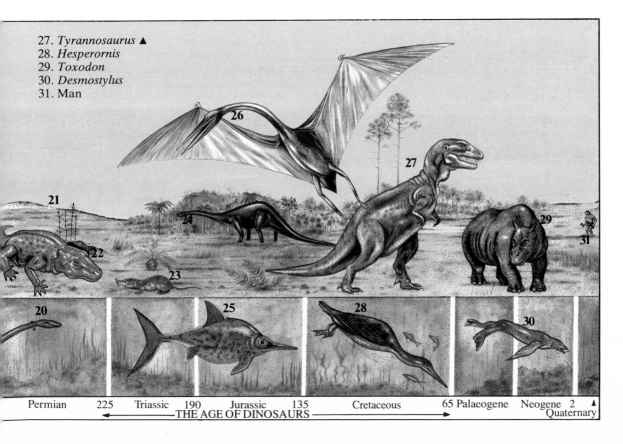

27. *Tyrannosaurus* ▲
28. *Hesperornis*
29. *Toxodon*
30. *Desmostylus*
31. Man

| Permian | 225 | Triassic | 190 | Jurassic | 135 | Cretaceous | 65 Palaeogene | Neogene 2 ▲ |

THE AGE OF DINOSAURS

Quaternary

# CLASSIFYING THE REPTILES

The vertebrates, the animals with backbones, belong to a number of distinct groups, or classes. In ascending order of evolutionary development, these are the fishes, the amphibians, the reptiles, and the birds and mammals at the top. It is the reptiles that interest us here.

A reptile can be defined as an animal that lays eggs on land, has no internal mechanism for controlling its body heat (that is, it is 'cold-blooded') and is covered with a scaly skin. The finer points of this definition do not apply to certain extinct groups, but for now it is a workable description. Modern reptiles include the snakes, the lizards, the crocodiles and alligators, the tortoises and turtles, and the strange tuatara of New Zealand. The reptiles do not play a very important part in today's fauna, but at one time, they were masters of the Earth.

The reptile class is subdivided according to the structure of the skull, and particularly the number of openings in it. The most primitive reptile skull has no openings in the side behind the eye socket. This is known as the *anapsid* condition and is found in the earliest reptiles, and in the tortoises and turtles of today.

Openings in the skull, behind the eye socket, developed later. These were to allow for the attachment of the various jaw muscles. The *synapsid* condition had a single opening low down. Animals showing this condition included the sail-backed pelycosaurs and the mammal-like reptiles, which eventually became the mammals.

In the *parapsid* condition, there is a single opening, high up on the skull. The great water reptiles of the Age of Dinosaurs had this type of skull, including the ichthyosaurs and the plesiosaurs. However, this may be just a coincidence. It now seems very likely that the ichthyosaurs and plesiosaurs evolved from stocks which were different from one another.

The largest reptile group has two openings on the side of the skull; this is the *diapsid* condition. This group includes the archosaurs, which is itself subdivided into the two orders of dinosaur (the Saurischia and the Ornithischia), the pterosaurs and the crocodiles. Also in this group are the snakes and lizards of the present day. It is from this group that today's birds are descended.

Although the reptiles were the most important actors on the evolutionary stage between the Carboniferous and the Cretaceous periods, they were by no means the only ones. Lesser roles were played by the mammals who had appeared by Triassic times. Birds, also, had developed by the upper Jurassic period. Fishes have always been abundant in the oceans and rivers and continued to be so throughout the rule of the reptiles on land. The amphibians had their major role in the Devonian and Carboniferous periods. Since then their significance has decreased.

*Euparkeria* was the kind of thecodont that evolved into the dinosaurs. Its two-footed stance was already dinosaur-like.

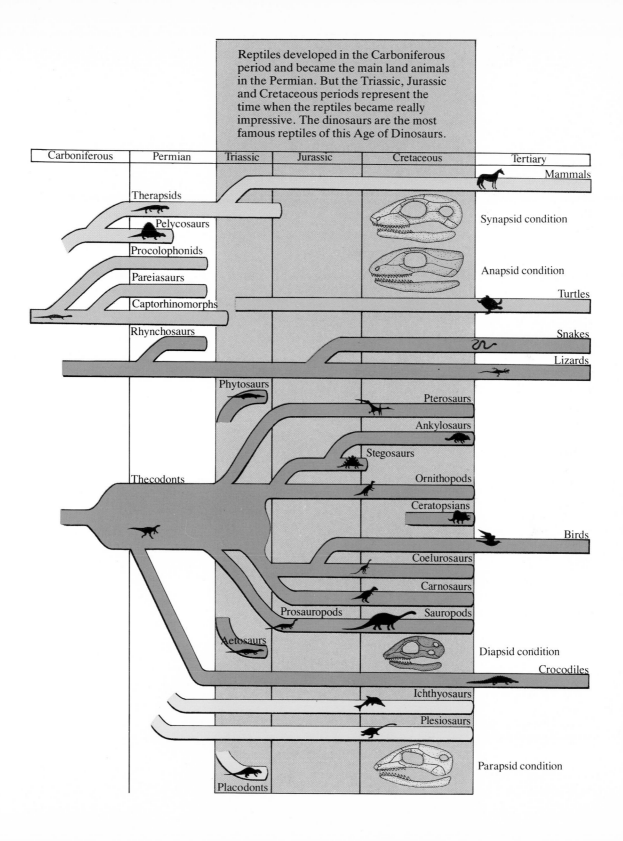

Reptiles developed in the Carboniferous period and became the main land animals in the Permian. But the Triassic, Jurassic and Cretaceous periods represent the time when the reptiles became really impressive. The dinosaurs are the most famous reptiles of this Age of Dinosaurs.

| Carboniferous | Permian | Triassic | Jurassic | Cretaceous | Tertiary |
|---|---|---|---|---|---|

Mammals

Therapsids

Pelycosaurs

Synapsid condition

Procolophonids

Pareiasaurs

Anapsid condition

Captorhinomorphs

Turtles

Rhynchosaurs

Snakes

Lizards

Phytosaurs

Pterosaurs

Ankylosaurs

Stegosaurs

Thecodonts

Ornithopods

Ceratopsians

Birds

Coelurosaurs

Carnosaurs

Prosauropods

Sauropods

Aetosaurs

Diapsid condition

Crocodiles

Ichthyosaurs

Plesiosaurs

Parapsid condition

Placodonts

# RUNNING AND FLYING

The shape of an animal and its lifestyle are interdependent. Different physical features in different animals adapt them to different environments. Animals that have the same lifestyles in similar environments tend to have similar features. It is almost as if nature has decided on a particular shape for a particular lifestyle, since a similar shape reappears time and time again in different animals. This is known as 'convergent evolution'.

The modern ostrich (*left*) and the Cretaceous *Struthiomimus* (*right*) lived in the same sort of landscape and had similar lifestyles. This much is obvious from the close similarity in size and shape between *Struthiomimus* and the ostrich.

If you look at animals that live in open country, for example, you will notice several similarities. Where there is no thick vegetation cover, there will be few places for an animal to hide. Hence, to escape a predator, an animal must run away from it; thus long legs are needed for a successful life on the open plains. Running legs have a particular shape. The muscles are concentrated at the top, working the rest of the leg by a system of tendons attached

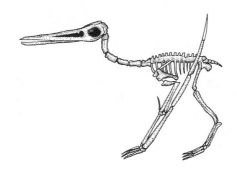
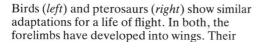

Birds (*left*) and pterosaurs (*right*) show similar adaptations for a life of flight. In both, the forelimbs have developed into wings. Their bodies are lightly built, and many of the bones are hollow. The skeletons shown here are of a pigeon and *Pterodactylus*.

to the bones. As a result the leg is long, thin and light, making it easy to move quickly. The thigh bone is short and strong to support the muscles, while the shin and foot bones are long and thin. In open country it is an advantage to see any potential enemy as soon as possible. A long neck gives an animal a good vantage point. It also enables the animal to reach food on the ground (for its long running legs mean that its body is some distance from the ground). The plains-dwelling creatures of today show all these features. The antelope and the ostrich are examples of this.

What works in the present day also worked in the past. We can look for these features in fossil animals and link them to their lifestyles. Dinosaurs such as *Struthiomimus* (page 82) had the long running legs and the long flexible neck. We can take this as an indication that this dinosaur, and others like it, lived in open country and was able to flee from approaching predators.

The adaptations for a flying mode of life are more obvious – wings are a necessity. However, the wings of a flying animal must be very light for them to function properly; hence such creatures have little in the way of hard parts that can be easily fossilized. Nevertheless, the fossilized imprints of the feathers of *Archaeopteryx* (page 60), the first bird, and the flying membranes of various pterosaurs have been found preserved in fine-grained rocks. Other features of these creatures which might become fossilized more easily enable us to identify them as fliers even from less complete remains.

The body of a flying animal must be lightweight. Both pterosaurs and birds have hollow bones that help to keep the body weight to a minimum. To this lightness, strength must be added and in both birds and pterosaurs many of the bones of the trunk are fused together giving a rigid inflexible support to the wing muscles. In both these groups of creatures the wings are supported by the forelimbs which are thus considerably longer and stronger than the hindlimbs. Moreover, an active flying life would need some form of body temperature control. Birds achieve this with their feathers; pterosaurs, we now know, were covered in fur, rather like bats.

The earliest pterosaur skeletons to be discovered in 1784 were thought to be those of a swimming animal. We would not make that mistake today.

The dolphin (1), shark (2) and ichthyosaur (3) all have streamlined bodies, a powerful swimming organ (flukes or fin) at the tail, and stabilizing organs on each side and on the back. They all eat fishes, and have the same lifestyle in the sea.

# SWIMMING AND BURROWING

The sea is another environment that requires a totally different set of adaptations from those needed for life on land.

All life on our planet came from the sea. The backboned animals that evolved in the sea evolved to fit into that environment exclusively. Their shape shows this. They had streamlined bodies to help them move through the water. They had fins to push against the water. Their teeth were suitable for eating others of their kind, or other sea-living creatures. These animals were the fishes, and today's fishes are built on exactly the same lines.

However, several groups of vertebrates, having left the sea and evolved successfully into land-dwelling creatures, returned to the sea later on in their history and adapted so well to their ancestral environment that their specialized body plan became very distinctive. Their bodies became long and torpedo-shaped, their limbs evolved into paddle-like organs, a powerful swimming fin developed on the tail, a stabilizing fin appeared on the back, and the jaws became long and full of small, pointed fish-catching teeth. This description matches that of the dolphin, a mammal that has long since abandoned its land-living existence and has taken up life in the sea again where it lives today. The description also applies to the ichthyosaur, a reptile which, by Triassic and Jurassic times, had done exactly the same thing. It could also be the description of a shark, however, a fish that evolved in the sea and whose shape has been so successful that it has remained practically unaltered for the past 400 million years.

The dolphin, the ichthyosaur and the shark have been quoted as excellent examples of convergent evolution.

Other sea-living reptiles have their mammal counterparts. The plesiosaurs (page 52), such as *Cryptocleidus*, probably lived very much as seals do today, chasing fishes through the oceans. The larger pliosaurs, such as *Peloneustes*, approached the size and appearance of today's whales.

Animals which lead a burrowing existence need physical adaptations which are similar to those that lead a swimming one. A streamlined body is necessary to ease its way through a dense medium. The animal moves along by movements of the body and the use of paddle-shaped limbs. Jaws full of small teeth enable the animal to eat other, smaller creatures in the same medium. The common moles of Europe and North America, the golden mole of southern Africa and the marsupial mole of Australia are almost identical in this respect. Again, these mammals are unrelated, merely showing the same adaptations to a similar lifestyle. The reptiles, also, are not without their 'moles'. Some of the skink lizards found in hot sandy areas show these features, and it is possible that the lengthening of the body and the reduction of the limbs for a burrowing way of life millions of years ago, gave rise to the snakes of today.

Burrowing and swimming are very similar. Any animal that lives in the ground needs to be streamlined to push its way through the soil. Moles (*left*) among the mammals, and skinks (*right*) among the reptiles show similar ground-swimming features.

# THE CHANGING SHAPE OF THE DINOSAUR

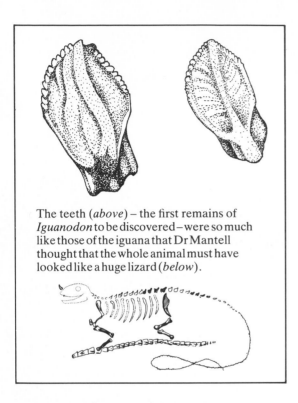

The teeth (*above*) – the first remains of *Iguanodon* to be discovered – were so much like those of the iguana that Dr Mantell thought that the whole animal must have looked like a huge lizard (*below*).

During the 1970s many people thought that the dinosaurs were warm-blooded animals, and led active lives like modern mammals and birds. This picture reflects this theory and shows *Iguanodon* as a very vigorous and energetic animal.

The restoration of an extinct animal from its scattered remains has never been easy. How much more difficult it must have been in the early days, before people knew anything about dinosaurs and the other great reptiles of long ago.

*Iguanodon* (page 74) was one of the first dinosaurs to be discovered. The first remains that came to light were a handful of teeth found by Mary, the wife of Dr Gideon Mantell, a keen fossil collector, in Sussex, England. This was back in 1822 when no-one had any idea of the age of the Earth, or of how it had changed through its history. The Bible Book of Genesis was the only guide to what happened long ago. The teeth puzzled Dr Mantell, and neither he nor other scientists of the time could decide which animal they came from. Eventually Dr Mantell recognized that the teeth, and others that he had found nearby, were very similar to those of the iguana lizard of South America. Hence he named his fossil animal *Iguanodon*, meaning 'iguana toothed'. By this time he had found some isolated bones as well as the teeth, and was able to attempt a restoration of the animal. Not surprisingly his drawing looked like a very large iguana. This restoration was accepted at the time and full-sized statues of it were built to stand in the grounds of the Crystal Palace in Sydenham, south London. They may be seen there to this day.

It was not until complete skeletons of *Iguanodon* were found that the true nature of the beast was seen. In 1878 the remains of over thirty *Iguanodon* were found in a mine at Bernissart in Belgium, and many of these were complete. For the first time it was seen that the animal walked on its hind legs, and had a head that was quite

small compared with the rest of the body. A bony spike, which Dr Mantell had placed on the nose of his animal, was seen to be the top joint of the thumb. The kind of restoration that was based on these remains has been the *Iguanodon* standard since that time.

In the 1970s the theory was put forward that dinosaurs were not cold-blooded reptiles after all, but were a group of animals that could regulate their body temperature, as do mammals and birds today (see page 27). This argues that they had an active lifestyle, and gave rise to some very different restorations, including one of *Iguanodon* racing across open country like a startled ostrich.

Even today, new evidence is being uncovered about the appearance of the fossil reptiles. The idea of cheek-pouches on the main restoration of *Iguanodon* is relatively new, suggested by the depressions in the sides of the skull, and the probable action of the teeth. As recently as 1983 fresh remains have shed more light on how the jaw worked, showing it to be much more complicated than originally thought.

New discoveries that show us something about the lifestyles of extinct animals are being made all the time, and no restoration can be regarded as totally accurate.

Most modern restorations show *Iguanodon* as a peaceful-looking two-footed herbivore supported by its tail. It probably used its thumb to help pull down branches and stripped off the leaves with its tongue and beak.

# RECONSTRUCTIONS AND RESTORATIONS

Sometimes we may be lucky enough to find a complete animal skeleton embedded in the rocks. Then we can see straight away what kind of animal has been discovered. Much more often, however, all we have are disjointed bones, and we have to compare them with more complete remains before they can be of use to us.

Fossil vertebrate bones can be extremely difficult to work with. They are liable to crumble away as soon as they are removed from their encasing rock, or on the way back from the site to the laboratory. To prevent such problems the exposed bone is wrapped in sacking soaked in plaster of Paris. When the covering is dry it protects the fossil while the remainder of it is removed from the rock. Then the whole bone is treated in the same way ready for its journey to the place of study. The position of each bone is noted accurately before its removal and this helps as a guide to the assembly of the whole skeleton later. If a mounted skeleton is to go on display then nowadays lightweight casts of the bones are made in glass-fibre for this purpose. The original fossils can then be kept for close study.

A mounted skeleton, as often seen in a museum, is called a *reconstruction* by palaeontologists. On the other hand, a *restoration* is a portrayal of what the entire animal would have looked like in life. A restoration can be a painting or a sculpture – or a photographic presentation, as in this book – and invariably is much more speculative than a reconstruction.

A restoration starts with a reconstruction. But even at this stage problems appear. It is more than likely that parts of the skeleton are missing, and the nature of the lost pieces must be worked out by looking at skeletons of related animals. The skulls of dinosaurs are unfortunately rarely preserved since their light construction makes them very vulnerable during the fossilization process.

By looking at the bones, palaeontologists can work out how the muscles were attached. The attachment points are often

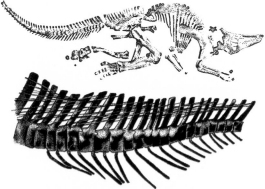

Fossil skeletons are only rarely found in as complete a form as this one of the duck-billed dinosaur *Anatosaurus* (top). When scientists find such a good one they can easily see what the animal looked like. Details of tendons attached to the bones (above) show, for example, that the tail was inflexible.

Usually a palaeontologist restoring a fossil animal has to guess what the skin was like. Sometimes, however, the actual skin is fossilized, if the animal has been buried quickly.

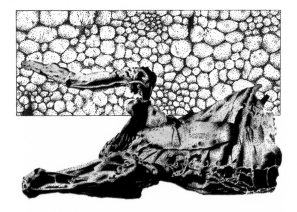

visible as scars on the bone's surface. We can tell if a part of the body, for example the tail, is flexible or stiff by looking at how the bones are arranged or joined together, and whether the joints have extra stiffening in the form of tendons.

Skin texture is usually a problem, as we do not often find fossilized skin. But fossil skin impressions may come to light where the animal has rolled in the mud and the mud has later hardened complete with the impression; or where the animal has died and the carcass dried, making the skin leathery and able to be fossilized.

One of the most speculative parts of a restoration is the colour scheme. There is hardly any direct evidence of the colour of an extinct animal. However, we can look at the colour schemes of today's animals and apply the same principles. We can give camouflage patterns to animals that need it, and make these patterns suitable for the kind of environment that they inhabited. As in today's animals, the larger creatures would have a more subdued colour and tend to be darker in overall tones, whereas the smaller creatures would be more brightly coloured.

The first job in restoration is to reconstruct the skeleton (1). Then we can work out where the muscles were attached (2). We can only guess at the colour (3) but, like most modern animals, *Anatosaurus* probably matched the landscape.

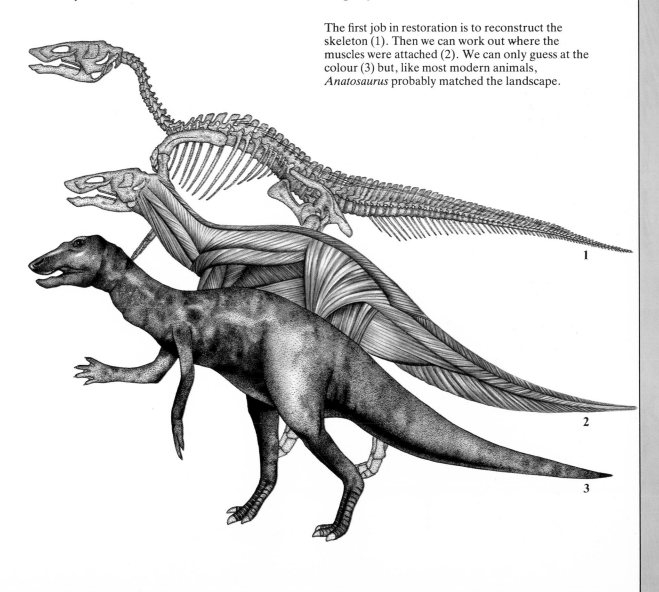

1

2

3

# THE DISCOVERIES

People have known about fossils for as long as they have been looking at the rocks. At first fossils were explained away as freaks of nature, or the Devil's handiwork placed there to test the faith of true believers in the biblical account of the Creation. Leonardo da Vinci 1452–1519, the great Italian artist, scientist and inventor, thought that fossil shells could be the remains of sea creatures. By the seventeenth century people widely accepted that fossils had once been alive, but they tended to use the biblical flood to account for their presence in rocks far from the sea.

It was in the early nineteenth century that dinosaur bones began to be recognized for what they really were. In 1822 Mary Mantell discovered the teeth that led to the unearthing of *Iguanodon* (pages 20 and 74). In 1824 Dean William Buckland of Oxford University discovered and described the bones of the meat-eating *Megalosaurus*, correctly identifying it as, and naming it, 'huge reptile'. In 1842 the British palaeontologist Richard Owen coined the name Dinosauria ('terrible reptiles') to apply to these and other similar remains. The term is no longer a scientific one but the word 'dinosaur' has slipped into popular use.

The hunt for fossil reptiles moved from Britain to the United States of America in 1855 when *Palaeoscincus* (page 86), one of the armoured dinosaurs, was discovered by Dr Ferdinand Vandiveer Hayden. In 1858 *Hadrosaurus*, one of the duck-billed dinosaurs (page 84), was unearthed by the Philadelphia anatomist Joseph Leidy.

Two American palaeontologists then began the hunt in earnest. Othniel Charles Marsh and Edward Drinker Cope were both wealthy men, and hired large teams to scour the continent for dinosaur remains. Unfortunately, there was no coop-

Othniel Charles Marsh (1831–99) was born in Lockwood, New York, and became Professor of Palaeontology at Yale University and vertebrate palaeontologist to the United States Geological Survey. His expeditions unearthed eighty new species of dinosaur.

eration between the two and, in fact, a deep rivalry grew between them. This drove each of them to make more and bigger finds than the other, with the result that by the beginning of the twentieth century many American museums had outstanding collections of fossil skeletons.

The focus of discovery then moved to Canada where in 1910 the fossil-hunter Barnum Brown of the American Museum of Natural History found the Red Deer River fossil site in Alberta.

Africa became a good hunting ground for fossil reptiles. As early as the 1860s prosauropod dinosaurs were found in South Africa. The mammal-like reptiles of that area of the Permian period were studied in great detail in the early 1900s by Robert Broom, a palaeontologist who had emigrated from Scotland. The most spectacular finds from that continent came from Tendaguru in present-day Tanzania. Between 1909 and 1929 German and British expeditions unearthed Jurassic dinosaurs that were similar to, and every bit as impressive, as those found by Cope and Marsh in North America.

Very often the best fossil animals are found in the most inhospitable of places, for example, the vast hostile Gobi Desert of Central Asia. In 1922 an expedition from the American Museum of Natural History, led by Roy Chapman Andrews, discovered bones there. His four later expeditions to that area turned up bones and nests of *Protoceratops*, a small horned dinosaur, as well as those of small flesh-

eating dinosaurs that preyed on them. Since the 1940s Russian expeditions have discovered vast graveyards of Cretaceous dinosaurs in Mongolia.

Further south, in China, there were a number of finds in the early twentieth century, but since 1950 and especially in the 1970s, a wealth of dinosaur remains have been discovered. Mostly from Shantung and Szechuan Provinces, these remains include the largest known duck-billed dinosaurs and sauropods with extremely long necks.

South America and Australia have also yielded the remains of fossil reptiles. These remains are very useful in showing how the continents have moved in relation to each other (page 8).

Since the 1960s there has been a great

Edward Drinker Cope (1840–97) was born in Philadelphia and studied there. His palaeontological expeditions were in direct competition with those of Marsh. Although he is best known for his work on Permian reptiles and Cenozoic mammals he also discovered fifty-six new species of dinosaur.

deal of new research on the subject, especially in the United States. New types of fossil reptile have been unearthed that would have been undreamed of in the early days of the science. These include the swift and fierce *Deinonychus* (page 76), discovered in 1964, and the vast pterosaur *Quetzalcoatlus* (page 80) found in 1971. Other discoveries cast light on the lifestyles of the ancient reptiles. For instance, hadrosaur nests unearthed in Montana in 1979 showed that the animals nested in extensive 'rookeries' and looked after their young for some time after birth.

Even more exciting than the actual study and description of the physical remains, are the new studies of how reptile physiology may have worked in times past. The biggest stir was caused in the early 1970s when it was suggested that the dinosaurs were endothermic; that is, they regulated their temperature by eating a great deal of food and having a high metabolic rate, like mammals and birds today. The evidence came largely from population studies that tried to show the proportions of meat-eating to plant-eating animals in a particular area where many

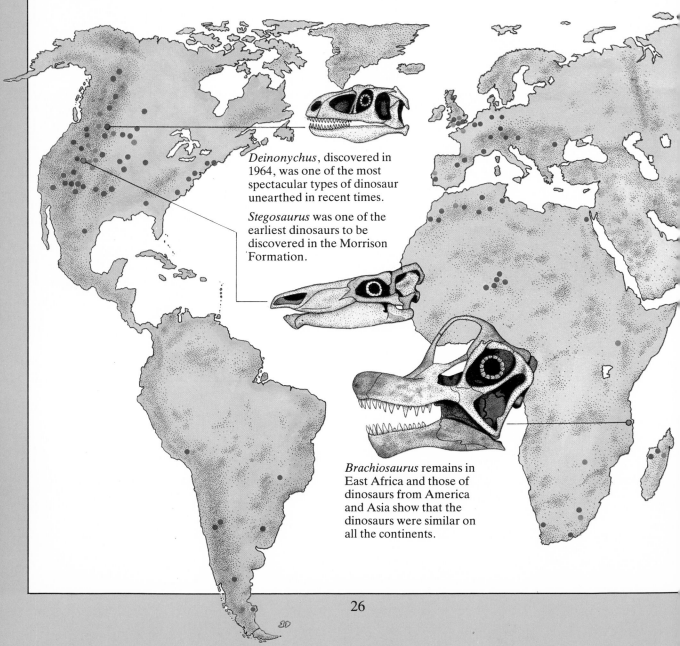

*Deinonychus*, discovered in 1964, was one of the most spectacular types of dinosaur unearthed in recent times.

*Stegosaurus* was one of the earliest dinosaurs to be discovered in the Morrison Formation.

*Brachiosaurus* remains in East Africa and those of dinosaurs from America and Asia show that the dinosaurs were similar on all the continents.

dinosaur remains have been found. A larger number of herbivores would be needed to feed a 'warm-blooded' meat-eater than would be needed to feed a 'cold-blooded' one. Such studies can only be approximate, though, since the amount of dinosaur remains found need not reflect the numbers and proportions of animals that actually lived at the time.

Another long-running matter of dispute has been about the dinosaurs' extinction. In the early days of the study of dinosaurs great disasters were blamed. These included the rise of mountain chains, widespread volcanic eruptions and great floods. Then general opinion swung towards a gradual process, giving as reasons the change in plant life, the change in climates and the movement of the continents. Suddenly in the early 1980s disasters were back in fashion. Mineralogical analyses of the topmost beds of the Cretaceous and the lowest beds of the succeeding Palaeogene suggested that there had been a massive meteor strike at this time. Such a strike would have sent up clouds of dust, blocking out the sun for several years and killing off the plant life.

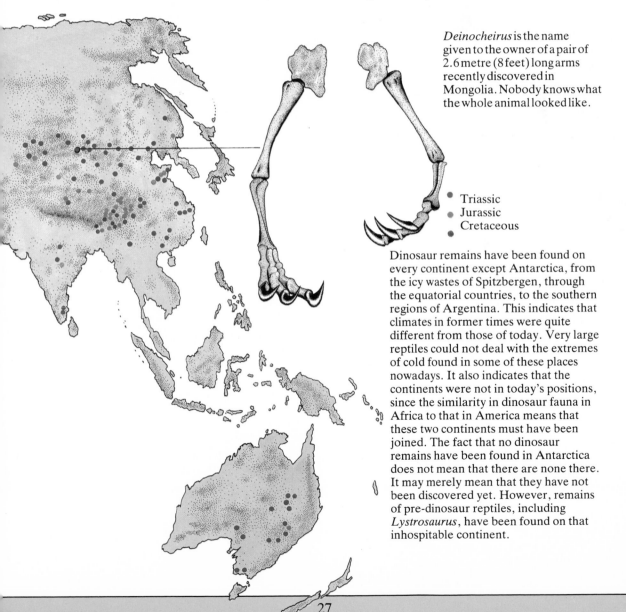

*Deinocheirus* is the name given to the owner of a pair of 2.6 metre (8 feet) long arms recently discovered in Mongolia. Nobody knows what the whole animal looked like.

● Triassic
● Jurassic
● Cretaceous

Dinosaur remains have been found on every continent except Antarctica, from the icy wastes of Spitzbergen, through the equatorial countries, to the southern regions of Argentina. This indicates that climates in former times were quite different from those of today. Very large reptiles could not deal with the extremes of cold found in some of these places nowadays. It also indicates that the continents were not in today's positions, since the similarity in dinosaur fauna in Africa to that in America means that these two continents must have been joined. The fact that no dinosaur remains have been found in Antarctica does not mean that there are none there. It may merely mean that they have not been discovered yet. However, remains of pre-dinosaur reptiles, including *Lystrosaurus*, have been found on that inhospitable continent.

# DINOSAUR LORE

The first serious attempt to bring the study of fossil animals before the general public took place in 1854. In that year the Crystal Palace was moved to its permanent site in the park at Sydenham, south London, after the Great Exhibition of 1851 for which the glass and steel structure had been built. It was Prince Albert who first suggested that the landscaped grounds of the park be populated with statues of extinct animals. The sculptor Waterhouse Hawkins was commissioned to build a number of statues of *Iguanodon*, *Megalosaurus* and several of the swimming and flying reptiles found in Britain. They were to be full-sized, built of brick covered with stucco, and standing in lifelike poses. The resulting statues were hopelessly inaccurate by today's standards, but a good attempt for the time. Their antique charm still attracts tourists to the park.

Waterhouse Hawkins then went to the United States in 1868, accepting a commission to construct similar statues for Central Park in New York. These were to be based on the studies of Joseph Leidy. Unfortunately, after three years' work, the project fell foul of local politics and was eventually abandoned.

By the turn of the century scientists had a much better idea of what extinct animals looked like than they did at the time of Waterhouse Hawkins. Yet up to the 1950s textbook illustrations tended to be very unimaginative. The same animals cropped up over and over again. *Tyrannosaurus*, *Diplodocus*, *Apatosaurus* (then called *Brontosaurus*), *Stegosaurus*, *Triceratops* and one or two others appeared with monotonous regularity. They were usually illustrated in the same lifeless poses, or as reproductions of the murals executed in the 1920s by the artist Charles R. Knight for the Field Museum of Natural History in Chicago. Another source of visual material consisted of photographs of the full-sized statues made by the sculptor A. Pallenberg in the grounds of Carl Hagenbeck's Hamburg zoo in the early 1900s. These statues were much more accurate than those of Waterhouse Hawkins. The successful and influential film *King Kong*, made in 1933, again called upon the services of the same few creatures. It was as if palaeontology had come to a complete halt after Cope and Marsh had finished their thorough work.

However, in the 1950s and 1960s there was a sudden upsurge, both of palaeontological research and of public interest in the subject. The renewed public interest meant a flood of books with artwork so badly executed that one yearned for the return of Charles R. Knight. 'Dinosaur parks' with glass-fibre models that looked absurd beside the now delapidated and bomb-damaged structures in Hagenbeck's zoo, made their appearance. Many films, making a mockery of the whole field of study, were turned out, quite insulting to the audience's level of knowledge.

We now seem to be coming out of that period. A new breed of fossil animal artists is coming forward, and better-informed books are being published. The more recently discovered animals are being portrayed and described.

In this book Jane Burton has photographed a very wide range of now-extinct reptiles. The animals are depicted in lifelike situations in accurate reconstructions of their habitats; each remarkable image is an exciting glimpse into the *real* Age of Dinosaurs.

# THE PHOTOGRAPHS

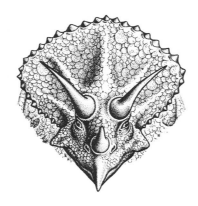

# HYLONOMUS

The coal forest is silent. Great trees of giant club-mosses stand, their roots spreading through the shallow water and mud, the green columns of their trunks obscuring one another as they stretch away across the seemingly endless expanse of humid swamp. Only a few rays of sunlight filter through the tree canopy, slanting down in misty shafts to dapple the mud and the undergrowth. Where the thick ooze of mud and decaying vegetation rises above the water's surface, a dense undergrowth of ferns and creeping horsetails spreads across it. Here and there a fallen tree-trunk lies in the water, embedded in the decaying plant debris that will eventually become coal. Trees have snapped off, their hollow stumps standing stark, slowly crumbling as their substance is eaten away by fungi and other agents of decay. In one such hollow stump there is a movement. A lizard-like head pops out and darts a look around. Then the whole animal, *Hylonomus*, scrambles over the moss and snaps up a small cockroach. It crunches the insect with its sharp teeth before swallowing it.

*H*ylonomus was one of the first reptiles. It resembled its amphibian ancestors in appearance, but there were some profound changes in its skeleton. The skull was a more robust structure than that of an amphibian and its limb girdles were much stronger. Unlike an amphibian, it did not have a moist skin. The most significant change, however, was in its reproduction. Amphibians laid eggs in water. These hatched into water-dwelling larval forms, or tadpoles, that only later grew into adult forms that could leave the water. *Hylonomus*, however, laid its eggs on land. These eggs were covered by a leathery protective shell that enabled the young to develop in their own private pools. They hatched out into individuals fully able to exist on dry land.

| HYLONOMUS | Length: 1m (3ft) | |
|---|---|---|
| Fossils: found in the Joggins Formation, at the base of the Upper Carboniferous | | |
| Locality: Nova Scotia | | |
| Order: Cotylosauria | Suborder: Captorhynomorpha | Family: Romeriidae |

The skeleton of *Hylonomus* shows a generalized shape much like that of a lizard today.

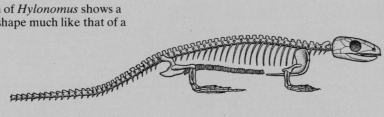

*Edaphosaurus* was typical of the plant-eating pelycosaurs of the Permian. It lived at the same time as *Dimetrodon* and was about the same size.

# DIMETRODON

There are deserts in Texas even in Permian times, 280 million years before man. The climate has been changing; the thick coal forest of a few million years before has turned to arid plains. Rainfall is sparse and the waterways and lakes are drying up. The great amphibians are dying out and the reptiles are spreading through the world. On a sandy mound above the early morning mists lies *Dimetrodon*, a great lizard-like creature with a strange-looking fin on its back. The dawn sun catches the full surface of the fin, warming it and the blood vessels that it contains. This warmth is transferred to the rest of the animal's body and, within an hour of the sun's rising, *Dimetrodon* will be active enough to waddle off in search of food. *Dimetrodon* is a meat-eater. Most of its contemporaries are meat-eaters too, or else eat fish and molluscs from the drying lakes and inland seas. Some of these reptiles also have a warming fin. Like *Dimetrodon* they lie facing the same direction, soaking up the sunlight. Soon they will scatter to the isolated clumps and thickets of ferns and horsetails to begin feeding. Other animals, without fins, will still be cold and sluggish at this hour – ideal prey for *Dimetrodon*!

*Dimetrodon* and the other fin-backed reptiles, such as the herbivorous *Edaphosaurus*, belonged to a group called the pelycosaurs. These were probably the first stage in the development of mammals from reptiles. Compared with the mammal-like reptiles which would evolve later, they had very few mammalian features. The meat-eating pelycosaurs, however, like mammals, had teeth of different sizes, with long teeth at the front and shorter teeth at the back.

The sail-like fin was probably an early stage in the development of 'warm-bloodedness', the ability of certain animals to adjust their own internal temperature and to remain active for longer periods. The fin was supported by long spines that grew from each vertebra of the back. The pelycosaurs were the most advanced and numerous of the large land animals at the beginning of the Permian period, but more sophisticated and spectacular creatures were to come.

| DIMETRODON | Length: 3.3m (11ft) |
|---|---|
| Fossils: found in Lower Permian Red Beds | |
| Locality: Texas and Oklahoma | |
| Order: Pelycosauria | Suborder: Sphenacodontia |

# LYCAENOPS

The sluggish rivers that weave their way across the vast arid interior of Gondwanaland in the Upper Permian provide welcome waterholes for the animals that wander the upland plains. One such is *Pareiasaurus*, a lumbering plant-eating reptile with a most unusual head covered with strange bony lumps. Having drunk its fill, it turns and climbs the bank towards a spot where succulent ferns are growing. Suddenly it is face to face with a *Lycaenops*. The smaller, mammal-like reptile, trotting along the bank, is just as startled as *Pareiasaurus*. For a moment each stands eyeing the other, until *Lycaenops* turns and lopes away. It has nothing to fear from the great plant-eater which it could easily kill if it were hungry. On another occasion the outcome might be different.

*L*ycaenops was one of the earlier mammal-like reptiles. Its body was quite dog-like in build and appearance, mainly because of the position of the legs. These were held under the body, so that the body's weight was over its feet. *Pareiasaurus*, on the other hand, showed the typical reptile arrangement of legs, with both pairs sticking out at the side so that the body was slung between them. Another feature of *Lycaenops*, which made it different from ordinary reptiles, was the arrangement of its teeth. It had long killing teeth at the front of the jaw, and shearing teeth at the back.

These advanced features made the mammal-like reptiles the most powerful and active meat-eaters of the time. The group was a wide one, the animals ranging in size from a few centimetres to some as large as cows. The larger ones tended to be plant-eaters, while the smaller ones were active hunters. Later forms became more and more mammal-like, but in the Permian period the more primitive forms were still sufficiently advanced to be the rulers of the Earth. The thecodonts, the ancestors of the dinosaurs, were a very unimportant group at this time.

| LYCAENOPS | Length: 1m (3ft) | |
| --- | --- | --- |
| Fossils: found in Upper Permian Beaufort sandstones | | |
| Locality: South Africa | | |
| Order: Therapsida | Suborder: Theridontia | Family: Gorgonopsia |

The mammal-like reptile (1) supported the weight of its body on top of straight legs held beneath it. A more typical reptile, like a lizard (2) has legs that sprawl sideways giving inefficient support.

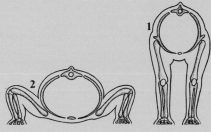

The skeleton of *Cynognathus* is typically
dog-like, particularly in the teeth and limbs.

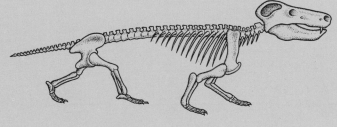

# CYNOGNATHUS

One of the most mammal-like of the mammal-like reptiles, *Cynognathus* has chased and brought down a plant-eating animal. Its cubs stayed near the den, resting out the hot afternoon in the shade of a conifer. Around them the sun beat down on the semi-arid Gondwanaland continent of the Lower Triassic. Now, towards evening, the adult *Cynognathus* has returned to feed the cubs, its stomach and mouth filled with meat which it has regurgitated for them. After the meal the young still gather round their parent, nosing its muzzle hoping for more food. They are very much part of a family group and it will be some time before they are old enough to take care of themselves.

The advanced mammal-like reptiles were hairy. We know this because their skulls have little pits that must have held whiskers, and whiskers are modified hairs. It seems likely that they also suckled their young, just as mammals do. The young were not born with a full set of teeth and would have needed their mother's milk when they were little. These creatures were probably warm-blooded; the hairy coat suggests this, and so does the presence of a palate. This shelf of bone separating the interior of the mouth and the nostrils meant that the animal could eat and breathe at the same time – a feature found in all warm-blooded animals that need a great deal of food and a constant supply of oxygen.

As in today's mammals, the teeth of these meat-eaters were arranged with nipping incisor teeth at the front, a pair of killing canine teeth, and shearing premolars and molars at the back. The arrangement of the legs was like that of a mammal too (page 35). With such a wealth of mammal-like features why are these creatures classed as reptiles? The hinging of the jaw provides the answer. This was still very primitive and typical of a reptile. The jaw structure had a number of bones that, in mammals, have become tiny and have been incorporated into the mechanism of the ear. Hence the ears of the mammal-like reptiles were also very primitive. The advanced mammal-like reptiles probably still laid eggs, but we cannot be sure about this. From this stage of development it was a very short step to the true mammals, a step taken later in the Triassic period.

| CYNOGNATHUS | Length: 2m (6½ft) | |
| --- | --- | --- |
| Fossils: found in Lower and Middle Triassic rocks | | |
| Locality: South African Karoo | | |
| Order: Therapsida | Suborder: Theriodontia | Family: Cynodontia |

# LYSTROSAURUS

Buoyed up by the surrounding water, a squat *Lystrosaurus* nimbly paddles its way across the bottom of an early Triassic river somewhere on the southern supercontinent of Gondwanaland. When it reaches the other side it will emerge slowly amid a growth of waterside vegetation so that, for a few moments, just its eyes and nostrils are exposed. Well hidden, it will establish that no threat is present before clambering into the shallows to browse on the water plants.

*Lystrosaurus* was one of the most specialized of the mammal-like reptiles. As a group these reptiles did not differ from one another much, each species tending to have the same basic shape and life habits. *Lystrosaurus*, however, was adapted to an amphibious existence just like the hippopotamus of today. Its clumsy-looking barrel-like body could be propelled gracefully underwater by limbs that could also support it on land, and its eyes and nostrils were placed close together on the top of its head, enabling the animal to breathe and look about while almost totally submerged. A pair of tusks pointing downwards from the upper jaw helped it to dig up from the mud the plants on which it fed. The tusks are characteristic of the group of mammal-like reptiles to which *Lystrosaurus* belonged – the dicynodonts, or the animals with two dog-like teeth – though they were all plant-eaters. *Lystrosaurus* fed on the few plants left of the *Glossopteris* seed-fern flora once common in Gondwanaland.

| LYSTROSAURUS | |
| --- | --- |
| Length: 1m (3ft) | Height at shoulder: 50cm (19in) |
| Fossil: found in freshwater Lower Triassic beds | |
| Locality: South Africa, India, Antarctica | |
| Subclass: Synapsida | Order: Dicynodontia |

*Lystrosaurus* and *Glossopteris* remains have been found in such diverse places as South Africa, India and Antarctica, supporting the theory that these continents were once joined together as Gondwanaland.

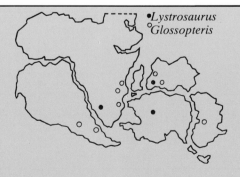

•*Lystrosaurus*
°*Glossopteris*

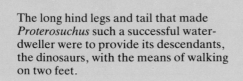

The long hind legs and tail that made *Proterosuchus* such a successful water-dweller were to provide its descendants, the dinosaurs, with the means of walking on two feet.

# PROTEROSUCHUS

Disturbed by the paddling of *Lystrosaurus* across the sluggish river, a sturgeon threshes its long body and swims out into mid-stream. Although the fish need not fear *Lystrosaurus*, danger lurks. Suddenly the scaly form of *Proterosuchus* rises from the murk of swirling silt and the animal's long jaws snap tightly on the hapless sturgeon. Trapped by a row of sharp teeth, the fish has no chance of escape. *Proterosuchus* sweeps its flattened tail, kicks its strong hind limbs and propels itself to the surface where it can eat at leisure.

*Proterosuchus* was one of the archosaurs, the second major group of reptiles living in the lower Triassic period 225 million years ago. While the mammal-like reptiles were the most important animals on land, the archosaurs took to the water – the territory patrolled by their amphibian ancestors. Their resemblance to today's crocodiles was more than just chance. The long jaws, the long body, the powerful flattened tail and strong hind legs made them well adapted to a swimming, fish- and flesh-eating existence. The crocodiles are direct descendants of the archosaurs and, indeed, this shape set the pattern for the major groups of land animals that would evolve later.

Once the mammal-like reptiles died out in the Triassic leaving only their mammal descendants, still insignificant at this stage, the archosaurs left the water. Most adopted a completely terrestrial lifestyle. Their long hind legs made it easy for them to take up a two-footed posture in which their bodies and heads were balanced by their long stiff tails. This is the basic shape of the descendants of *Proterosuchus*, the thecodonts, who in turn gave rise to the bipedal early dinosaurs. Other archosaur offshoots include the pterosaurs, adapted to a life of flight, and the crocodiles, which retained their ancestors' aquatic habits – so successfully that they remain unchanged to this day.

| PROTEROSUCHUS | Length: 1.5m (5ft) |
|---|---|
| Fossils: found in Lower Triassic freshwater deposits | |
| Locality: Africa | |
| Order: Thecodontia | Suborder: Proterosuchia |

41

# PODOPTERYX AND LONGISQUAMA

From the trunk of a tall tree fern a small *Podopteryx* launches itself into the air. It spreads its limbs and suddenly changes from what appeared to be an ordinary tree-climbing lizard into a swooping airborne creature. It catches currents of air in a membrane of skin stretched between its hind legs and tail and along its sides, gliding towards the lower branches of a nearby conifer. But *Longisquama*, another lizard-like tree dweller, is already there. In alarm, *Longisquama* raises the crest of elongated scales along its back in a warning display which makes *Podopteryx* bank away to find another perch.

Both these creatures were thecodonts and may represent the ancestral stocks of some of the well-known flying animals which would evolve later. They lived on the forested lowlands of the south-eastern corner of the supercontinent of Laurasia, by the shores of the Tethys Ocean. *Podopteryx* may have been an ancestor of the pterosaurs, with their flying membranes supported by their limbs. In this early pattern, however, the arrangement of the main part of the membrane attached to the hind legs and tail must have limited it to a gliding rather than a flying action. The later pterosaurs had the membrane attached to the elongated forelimbs, so could achieve far more control over their movements.

*Longisquama* represents a very different line altogether. Its main feature was the erectile crest of long scales, V-shaped in section, which could be folded along its back when at rest. The remainder of its body was covered with overlapping scales that were strongly keeled. It is thought that these specialized scales represent an early stage in the evolution of feathers, and so this line of animals could possibly have developed into the birds.

| PODOPTERYX | LONGISQUAMA |
|---|---|
| Length: 30cm (1ft) | Length: 15cm (6in) |
| Fossils: found in Middle Triassic lake deposits | Locality: Osh, Soviet Kirgizstan |
| Order: Thecodontia | Suborder: Pseudosuchia |

Another reptilian flying experiment,
took place in the Late Triassic of Europe,
that of *Kuehneosaurus*, which glided on
wings supported by extended ribs.

This is a complete adult nothosaur
skeleton with two young.

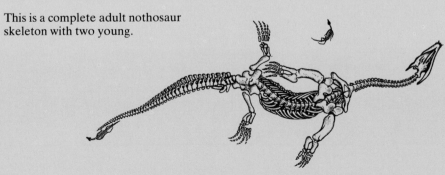

# NOTHOSAURUS AND TANYSTROPHEUS

A sudden squall whips over the inland sea that reaches across the area of central Europe in Middle Triassic times. The squall passes, but the waves it has caused spread over the sea to beat and plunge against the cliffs and rocks of a chain of islands. The sea reptiles cluster on the rocks, squabbling. They are all fish-eaters and are watching for the turbulent water to settle, when the fish will return to feed near the shoreline. Several *Nothosaurus* wait on the rocks for the sun to come out again and warm their bodies, chilled by the sudden shower. A group of *Tanystropheus* weave their long necks as they watch two *Nothosaurus* fence with open jaws.

The skeletons of these creatures, and other more lizard-like forms, have been found in deposits that were laid down in sea caves during the Middle Triassic period. The nothosaurs, to which *Nothosaurus* belonged, were long-toothed swimming reptiles and were ancestors to the plesiosaurs. A widespread group, they ranged in length from 30 centimetres (1 foot) to 6 metres (19 feet). They were one of the first reptile groups whose bodies had adapted for a return to the sea. These specializations were the beginnings of paddled feet, a fin on the tail and teeth adapted for fish-catching. *Tanystropheus*, with its absurdly long neck, posed a problem for palaeontologists. At first only the neck bones were discovered and these were so long that they were thought to be limb bones. Only when a full skeleton was found did the animal reveal itself to be a lizard with a 3 metre (10 feet) long neck. This probably helped *Tanystropheus* to reach for fish in rockpools.

| NOTHOSAURUS | Length: 3m (10ft) |
|---|---|
| Fossils: widespread around the area of the Late Triassic Tethys Ocean and its surrounding shelves and inlets | |
| Localities: England, the Netherlands, Switzerland, Poland, Germany, Tunisia, Israel, Jordan, India, Japan and China | |
| Order: Sauropterygia | Suborder: Nothosauria |
| TANYSTROPHEUS | Length: 4m (13ft) |
| Fossils: found in Middle Triassic cave deposits in hollows in Devonian limestone | |
| Locality: south-west Poland | Order: Protorosauria |

# SALTOPUS

In the cool Triassic desert night, in the arid uplands where Scotland now lies, *Saltopus*, a tiny dinosaur, built like a small chicken, scampers through the sand, stopping and listening every now and again for movement that might indicate food. There is a scrabbling among the rocks – and *Saltopus* pounces, darting out its long neck to catch the unwary creature. The squirming victim is a *Morganucodon*, a small mammal. Suddenly the *Saltopus* is disturbed, caught in a flash of light – it turns and, still with its furry mouthful, scampers off into the night.

*Saltopus* was one of the smallest of the dinosaurs and a member of the Procompsognathidae, the earliest and most primitive of the flesh-eating dinosaurs known as theropods. In appearance it resembled some of its ancestors, the bipedal thecodonts. However, the hips were more firmly anchored to the backbone, greatly strengthening the back legs and enabling the animal to walk exclusively on its hind feet. This left the hands free for grasping and they began to develop a standard three-clawed arrangement. In *Saltopus*, however, there were still five fingers on each hand, although the fourth and fifth were tiny and practically useless.

Remains of procompsognathids have been found in northern Europe and eastern North America, which were joined together in a single land mass in Upper Triassic times. More often than bones and skeletons, their remains consist of rows of footprints left in the desert sandstones as the animals left the arid areas, and moved about on the damp sands at the edges of oasis waterholes and inland seas. The three-toed footprints are remarkably like those of birds, and were often described as such when they were discovered in the early part of the nineteenth century.

*Morganucodon* was one of the earliest mammals. The mammals that evolved during the Triassic period remained unspecialized little insectivores, not unlike today's shrews, throughout the 150 million year reign of the dinosaurs.

| | | |
|---|---|---|
| SALTOPUS | Length: 60cm (2ft) | Height at hips: 20cm (8in) |
| Fossils: found in the Upper Triassic Stagonolepis Sandstone | | |
| Locality: Elgin, Scotland | | |
| Order: Saurischia | Suborder: Theropoda | Family: Procompsognathidae |

Many procompsognathid footprints were found in the Triassic sandstones of Connecticut in the early nineteenth century and their origin attributed to birds.

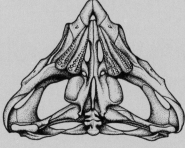

The underside of the skull of *Hyperodapedon* shows well the beak and the double row of teeth at the back of the jaw.

# HYPERODAPEDON

The sun scorches down on the arid uplands of the Upper Triassic northern continent. Here and there, in the hollows and valleys, temporary pools remain for a while after the rainy season. Around them grow beds of horsetails. Moving slowly among the thin vegetation, a pair of *Hyperodapedon*, dun-coloured and well-camouflaged against the sand and yellow rocks, browse on the plants. One uses its curved beak to nip off the growing shoots, chops them up with the scissor-like teeth at the back of its jaw, and swallows them down into its barrel-shaped body for a long digestion period.

*H*yperodapedon was one of the rhynchosaurs, a group of plant-eating reptiles that flourished briefly during Triassic times. Before them, during the Permian period, the mammal-like reptiles were the most important land animals, but these began to dwindle in number at the beginning of the Triassic. This may have been due to the fact that the *Glossopteris* seed-fern flora upon which the mammal-like reptiles fed changed at this time, one type of seed fern giving way to another. As these creatures died out the rhynchosaurs multiplied and took their place as the main herbivores. By the end of the Triassic the vegetation had changed again, this time to one consisting principally of conifers. The rhynchosaurs died out and were replaced by the descendants of the archosaur group, the dinosaurs.

In *Hyperodapedon* the front bones of the skull had developed into a hooked beak. Its back teeth were in double rows in the upper jaw, with the teeth of the lower jaw fitting between the rows like a penknife blade into its slot. This arrangement would have been excellent for snipping and chopping vegetation. *Hyperodapedon*'s deep body would have held a large digestive system that could have coped with large quantities of tough plant material. The rhynchosaurs were related to the present-day tuatara of New Zealand. The tuatara is the only surviving member of this once-abundant group of Triassic reptiles.

| | |
|---|---|
| HYPERODAPEDON | Length: 1.3m (4ft) |
| Fossils: found in Upper Triassic Lossiemouth Sandstone | |
| Locality: North-east Scotland | |
| Order: Rhynchocephalia | Family: Rhynchosauria |

# THECODONTOSAURUS

It is the rainy season in Upper Triassic times, and the limestone hills that stretch from Wales into northern Germany have a sparse covering of seasonal vegetation. Rivers gush and gurgle in chasms that are dry for most of the year. Along the edge of one a pair of *Thecodontosaurus* forage among the ferns and cycads. Sometimes on two legs, sometimes on four, these prosauropod dinosaurs seek their food on the ground and in the trees. Although they can eat meat, and can snap up lizards and large insects with a dart of the neck, their teeth are not so sharp, nor so pointed, as those of their thecodont ancestors. They can just as easily feed on leaves and tender shoots from the trees and herbs. Food is plentiful for the moment, by the damp gorge, but soon it will be the dry season. Then they will descend to the plains and migrate towards the shallow limy sea that edges the great Tethys Ocean to the south and east. There, where the climate is less harsh, they will remain until the rainy season comes again and they can return to their hills.

The prosauropods as a group were among the first of the dinosaurs to adopt a plant-eating way of life. Indeed, these animals were an in-between stage as the swift meat-eating thecodonts evolved into the huge, lumbering plant-eating sauropods that were to be so characteristic of the following period, the Jurassic. The smaller and more primitive prosauropods, such as *Thecodontosaurus*, could eat both meat and plants, but some of the later ones, such as *Riojasaurus*, became very large and were purely herbivorous. *Thecodontosaurus* remains have been found in ancient cave deposits in the region of Bristol in western England. The caves were eroded into Carboniferous limestone in Triassic times. Triassic animals sheltered in these caves and their bones became buried there when they died. Further to the east, in Germany, the Triassic sandstones contain large numbers of prosauropod footprints, all heading in the same direction. These probably show that the animals moved in herds, along seasonal migration routes. Although the prosauropods normally walked on hind legs, like their ancestors, they could also move about on all fours.

| | |
|---|---|
| THECODONTOSAURUS | Length: 2m (6½ft) |
| Fossils: found in Upper Triassic Keuper marl | |
| Locality: Western and central England, and possibly South Africa and northern Australia | |
| Order: Saurischia<br>Infraorder: Prosauropoda | Suborder: Sauropodomorpha<br>Family: Thecodontosauridae |

The prosauropod shape (2) shows the
group to have been a stage of
development between the thecodonts (1)
and the sauropods such as *Apatosaurus* (3).

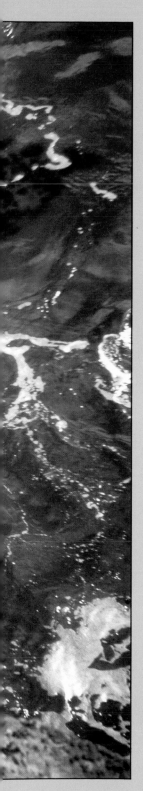

# CRYPTOCLEIDUS

It is the Upper Jurassic period and shallow seas cover most of northern Europe. Beneath the headlands of ancient metamorphic rock that jut up along the north coast of the island stretching from London to Belgium, a number of reptiles are swimming. As the waves suck and gurgle around the rocky ledges, a group of small plesiosaurs, *Cryptocleidus*, paddle lazily on the surface. Their long necks keep their heads above the water, enabling them to breathe, but now and again they dip their heads beneath the surface and dart at a passing fish. Suddenly a dark shape drifts into view below. It is *Peloneustes*, one of the very large short-necked plesiosaurs. *Peloneustes* is hunting ammonites and other cephalopods and is harmless to the *Cryptocleidus* group. Nevertheless, the smaller plesiosaurs are startled and they turn to swim swiftly away.

The plesiosaurs were a very widespread, varied and successful group of swimming reptiles. Descended from the same stock as the nothosaurs, they developed early in the Jurassic into two main lines. The first group, the elasmosaurs, were described by Dean William Buckland in the early days of vertebrate palaeontology as 'snakes threaded through turtles'. Indeed, the most noticeable feature of these animals was their snaky necks. *Cryptocleidus* was one of the smaller of the elasmosaurs but some of the Upper Cretaceous types, such as *Elasmosaurus*, grew to lengths of 10 metres (32 feet).

The second group of plesiosaurs were the pliosaurs. These had very big heads with short necks and their bodies reached immense sizes. Pliosaurs like *Peloneustes* lived rather like today's toothed whales, feeding mainly on large cephalopods. The diet of the plesiosaur group is well known from fossils of their stomach contents.

| CRYPTOCLEIDUS | Length: up to 3m (10ft) |
|---|---|
| Fossils: found in Upper Jurassic Oxford Clay | |
| Locality: central England | |
| Order: Sauropterygia | Suborder: Plesiosauria |

The many-toothed jaws and long neck of *Cryptocleidus* were ideal for catching fishes.

# METRIORHYNCHUS

Looking up through the sparkling waters of a northern European sea, we glimpse the silhouette of the ocean crocodile *Metriorhynchus*, chasing shoals of fishes with a weave and a dash that makes the reptile resemble a fish itself. This is one of several of the reptiles of Jurassic times that has broken with the lifestyle of its terrestrial ancestors and has returned to a completely aquatic way of life.

The earliest true crocodiles belonged to a group called the Mesosuchia and lived in the sea. At first glance they resembled the fish-eating gavials of the present day with their long slender muzzles and their needle-like teeth. Their legs were short and their toes webbed, and there was a double row of bony plates down the middle of the back.

However, a few types of crocodile departed widely from this general pattern and formed a thoroughly ocean-going group known as the Thalattosuchia. *Metriorhynchus* was a perfectly adapted marine form of this group. Its ancestors underwent the same sorts of changes that the ancestors of the ichthyosaurs passed through to turn them from land-dwelling reptiles to creatures fully at home in the sea. The four stout legs were replaced by swimming paddles, the rear pair more powerful than the forelimbs. The body itself became long and sinuous. Streamlined and completely smooth, it did not have the bony plates of its relatives. The tail, instead of being flattened along its whole length, turned down at the end to support a triangular swimming fin.

It is not known whether the thalattosuchians were sufficiently well adapted to marine life to bear their young alive, as did the ichthyosaurs. Their fish-like shape, however, enabled them to twist and dash after their fish prey in the warm seas that covered much of northern Europe in middle Jurassic times. They were as completely adapted in their shape to life in water as the descendant of a land animal could be.

| METRIORHYNCHUS | Length: 3m (10ft) |
|---|---|
| Fossils: found in Middle Jurassic Oxfordian beds | |
| Locality: Europe, South America | |
| Order: Crocodilia | Suborder: Thalattosuchia |

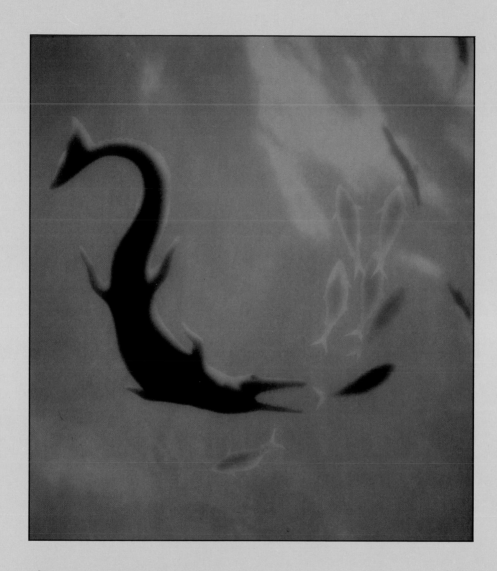

The modern crocodile (2) still resembles its semi-aquatic Triassic ancestors while *Metriorhynchus* (1) demonstrates a more specialized shape suited for its marine life-style.

The fish-like shape of the ichthyosaur is often shown where its body tissues have been partially preserved with the skeleton.

# OPHTHALMOSAURUS

A shoal of silvery fishes weaves and darts in the warm shallow sea of Upper Jurassic northern Europe. Above them looms a family group of *Ophthalmosaurus*, most elegant and streamlined of the fish-like reptiles or ichthyosaurs. Sunlight shafts through the fine suspension of silt carried from distant river mouths. The reptiles dawdle away the watery noon, waiting for the light to fade. They are crepuscular animals, feeding at dusk and dawn, their huge eyes enabling them to locate sleeping fishes lying on the bottom or nocturnal invertebrates creeping out of cracks in the reef.

The ichthyosaurs were the most successful group of reptiles to recolonize the ocean. Their bodies had become streamlined, their legs evolved into paddles and their tails developed a powerful swimming fin. By the Upper Jurassic period the changes had culminated in *Ophthalmosaurus* whose perfect adaptation to an aquatic life matched that of the sharks or today's dolphins, even to the triangular stabilizing dorsal fin. Because *Ophthalmosaurus* was so dolphin-like it has always been assumed that it lived by catching fish. But unlike earlier ichthyosaurs, *Ophthalmosaurus* had no teeth. Without long or sharp teeth, how did it capture fast-manoeuvring slippery prey? *Ophthalmosaurus* had huge eyes supported by a ring of bone that helped withstand changes in pressure. It could have hunted by sight in dimly lit water, taking sleeping or slower-moving prey.

The ichthyosaur body outline is well known, since the shape of the whole animal has often been found in the Lower Jurassic shales of Germany. Preserved as a thin film of carbon, these fossils show the position of fins and other soft parts. Such detailed remains even show the animal giving birth to live young, proving that it never needed to come ashore to lay eggs. Even the skin tissues can be examined to find the pigmentation cells. The ichthyosaur skin was tortoiseshell coloured.

| OPHTHALMOSAURUS | Length: 3m (10ft) |
|---|---|
| Fossils: found in the Upper Jurassic Oxford Clay | |
| Locality: England | |
| Subclass: Ichthyopterygia | |

# COMPSOGNATHUS

Scampering through the lush undergrowth, a pair of *Compsognathus* dart like active lizards. The female has caught a bright red dragonfly, and the male is trying to snatch it from her before she can swallow it whole. Through horsetail thickets and among gingko saplings they chase, until the male gives up and leaves his mate in peace to finish her meal. Their home is the cycad and gingko forest that covers the scattering of islands in the Upper Jurassic lagoons of Germany. Above the trees and away out over the quiet waters the pterosaurs flap and wheel while on a nearby wooded island *Archaeopteryx*, the first bird and a very close relative of *Compsognathus*, adds its squawks to the buzzing and rustling sounds of the still morning.

*Compsognathus*, the size of a domestic hen, was the smallest known of the meat-eating coelurosaur dinosaurs. Only two skeletons have been found, but from these it is obvious that it was an active hunter of smaller animals. The best known of the two fossil skeletons was found in the lithographic limestone of Germany. This limestone is remarkable for its ability to preserve skeletons to the finest detail. The bones of a lizard in the area of the stomach give evidence of the diet of *Compsognathus*. This coelurosaur had three toes on its long hind legs, as did other coelurosaurs, but it was unusual in having only two fingers on each hand. In this way the smallest of the meat-eating dinosaurs resembled *Tyrannosaurus*, which was the largest.

| COMPSOGNATHUS | Length: 60cm (2ft) |
|---|---|
| Fossils: found in the Upper Jurassic Lithographic Limestone | |
| Locality: Bavaria and south-east France | |
| Order: Saurischia<br>Infraorder: Coelurosauria | Suborder: Theropoda<br>Family: Coeluridae |

Like other complete dinosaur skeletons, that of *Compsognathus* was found with its head twisted back and its tail pulled up – a position taken up as the tendons of the spine dried and shrank after death.

The few specimens of *Archaeopteryx* so
far found show a dinosaur-like skeleton,
but the fossils are preserved in such fine
limestone that the feathers are very clear.

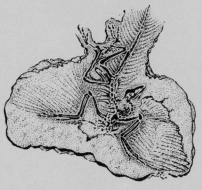

# ARCHAEOPTERYX

The wooded islands scattered across the central European lagoons in Upper Jurassic times are teeming with animal life. Insects scuttle and leap through the undergrowth, safe from the flapping pterosaurs that cannot manoeuvre in the thick vegetation. Yet there are other predators among the foliage. A sharp-eyed *Archaeopteryx* flutters down, its wings still outspread, and scampers amid the ferns and flurries of gingko leaves after a flying locust.

*A*rchaeopteryx is regarded by some palaeontologists as the first bird, and by others as a feathered dinosaur. In any case it seems to have been a creature in between the two groups. The skeleton was almost identical to that of the little coelurosaur *Compsognathus*, yet it was covered in feathers. In fact, the arrangement of feathers was identical to that of modern birds. Unlike the birds of today, however, *Archaeopteryx* had teeth in its jaws, claws on its wings and a long bony tail – all features showing that its immediate ancestors were reptiles. For all its fine feathers *Archaeopteryx* was not a good flyer, and certainly not as good as the contemporary pterosaurs. Although the bones were hollow and light, its muscles were weak. The creature may have lived in the trees taking occasional fluttering glides to the ground.

We know about *Archaeopteryx* from five skeletons and a single feather fossilized in the very fine lithographic limestone of Bavaria. This limestone is so fine that it preserves the traces of the finest organisms fossilized in it, from the legs of shrimps to pterosaur flying membranes. Without the discovery of the feathers the creature would have been identified as a dinosaur. The fossils provide proof that the birds were descended from the dinosaurs but, curiously, it was the lizard-hipped, rather than the bird-hipped, dinosaurs which were their ancestors.

| ARCHAEOPTERYX | Length: 30cm (1ft) | Weight: 500gm (18oz) |
|---|---|---|
| Fossils: found in the Upper Jurassic Lithographic Limestone | | |
| Locality: Solenhofen, southern Germany | | |
| Order: Aves | | |

# PTERODACTYLUS

The sun rises over the broad shallow lagoons that cover much of southern Germany in Upper Jurassic times. The first rays rouse the early morning insects that skim across the surface of the placid waters. From the surrounding stands of cycads and conifers, there swoops a small broad-winged pterosaur – *Pterodactylus*. With powerful strokes of its membranous wings it descends towards the water surface. Then, using the stretch of its hindlimbs to control its flight, it turns, snatches a dragonfly from the air and flaps its way back to the trees.

*Pterodactylus* was about the size of a pigeon although its wings, being less efficient than birds' wings, were proportionally larger. The ability of creatures to fly had improved greatly since the time of the *Pterodactylus* ancestor *Podopteryx*. The wings of *Pterodactylus* were supported on elongated and thickened fourth fingers, the bones of which were as thick as those of the limb itself. Like those of birds, the limb bones were hollow. The effective area of each wing could be controlled by the spread of the hind limbs, stretching the membranes to the fullest extent on the downstroke to catch as much air as possible, and narrowing them on the upstroke to reduce the air resistance. The body and limbs of *Pterodactylus* and the other pterosaurs were covered by a fine fur, indicating that these creatures had some sort of body heat control, like today's mammals and birds. This would have given them the energy needed for an active life of flight among the forests, swamps and mountains of the Mesozoic supercontinents.

The pterosaurs formed two suborders: the Pterodactyloidea to which *Pterodactylus* belonged; and the more primitive Rhamphorynchoidea. The latter group had narrower wings and a long stiff tail. The diets of the various types of pterosaur varied, as can be seen by their different teeth patterns. Pterosaurs were widespread and their remains have been found on all present-day continents except Antarctica.

| PTERODACTYLUS | |
|---|---|
| Wingspan: 25cm (10in) | Length: 22cm (9in) |
| Fossils: found in the Upper Jurassic Lithographic Limestone | |
| Locality: Solenhofen, southern Germany | |
| Order: Pterosauria | Suborder: Pterodactyloidea |

We can tell the diet of pterosaurs, and other animals, by looking at their teeth. *Pterodaustro* (1) scooped plankton from the water, *Anurognathus* (2) ate insects, *Dimorphodon* (3) ate meat, and *Pteranodon* (4) caught fishes.

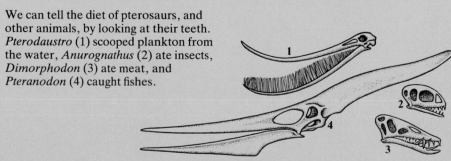

The skull of *Apatosaurus* was always
assumed to be square and box-like.
When one was finally discovered in 1979,
it was found to be quite long and
slender, similar to that of *Diplodocus*.

# APATOSAURUS

The rain stops and the clouds pass. The surfaces of the shallow backwaters and creeks return to stillness. From the damp forest that clothes the river banks and sandspits a herd of *Apatosaurus* emerges. Tall necks swaying from side to side, the great creatures lumber down the shingle bar to ease themselves into the water.

Away to the west the rain is still falling upon the infant Rocky Mountains. The stony material worn away from their crags and peaks is washed down by mountain rivers and spread out on a vast low-lying plain between the mountains and the sea. Rivers and streams meander here, between the newly deposited banks and bars of sand and shingle. 150 million years later all this material will become the complex of sandstones, conglomerates and shales that will cover great areas of the United States from Montana to New Mexico, and will be called the Morrison Formation. For now, however, this is an environment of still and sluggishly moving water. The banks support a steaming vegetation of cycads, tree ferns and gingkoes. Here and there are stands of taller conifers and by the edges of the swampy pools grow thick beds of horsetails. It is a lush environment that can support a large number of large plant-eating animals.

*A*patosaurus roamed the forested plains and swamps in herds, but it probably spent most of its existence in the shallow waters. Tracks of footprints show that the animal's huge body was completely buoyed up by the water as it clawed its way along using its forelimbs only. The tiny peg-like teeth were ideal for raking up the soft water weeds and the great sweep of the neck meant that the animal could reach a large area of aquatic plants without moving from one spot. *Apatosaurus* moved from one area of water to another in family groups, with the young protected in the middle.

*Apatosaurus* was once known scientifically as *Brontosaurus*, and still is in popular terms. *Apatosaurus* (meaning 'headless lizard', because the early specimens found lacked the skull) was the name first given to the animal and so it is accepted as a scientific name.

---

APATOSAURUS

| | | |
|---|---|---|
| Length: 20m (65ft) | Weight: 30 tonnes | |
| Fossils: found in Upper Jurassic Morrison Formation | | |
| Locality: Colorado | | |
| Order: Saurischia | Infraorder: Sauropoda | Family: Atlantosauridae |

# DIPLODOCUS

Stands of conifers are dotted about the Upper Jurassic swamp, isolated from the surrounding forest by the meanderings of the rivers. In the noonday shade cast by these great trees a herd of *Diplodocus* is seen. Normally they are down by the water raking up floating plant material with their peg-like teeth. Now they sample the undergrowth and the delicate new shoots from high up in the trees. From ground level their immensely long necks appear to be as high as the huge trees themselves, but this is only a trick of perspective. Like the *Apatosaurus* herds wading nearby, *Diplodocus* live in family groups. They move from one feeding ground to another with the young protected in the middle. Once the midday heat has passed they will move down to the water again and immerse themselves in the warm shallows, scooping about for water plants.

*D*iplodocus and its relatives were much longer and more lightly built than their *Apatosaurus* cousins. Although *Diplodocus* was so much longer than *Apatosaurus* it was only about one-third of its weight. Its backbone consisted of vertebrae that were made of struts and hollows, combining great strength with lightness. Tall spines pointed upwards from the vertebrae over the hips, supporting the muscles used for moving the hind legs and the tail. The tail vertebrae had downward projecting arms with skids at the ends. These probably protected the nerves and blood vessels of the tail as it dragged on the ground. The feet were armed with strong claws, three on the hind feet and one on the front, to prevent the animal from slipping in the mud of the swamps. *Diplodocus* may have swallowed stones to help grind up food inside the gizzard, since its teeth would not have been able to do much chewing.

| DIPLODOCUS | Length: 28m (91ft) | |
| --- | --- | --- |
| Fossils: found in Upper Jurassic Morrison Formation | | Locality: Utah |
| Order: Saurischia<br>Infraorder: Sauropoda | Suborder: Sauropodomorpha<br>Family: Atlantosauridae | |

The 28 metre length of *Diplodocus* included 14 metres of tail and 8 metres of neck. It stood 4 metres high at the hips.

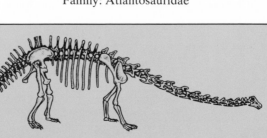

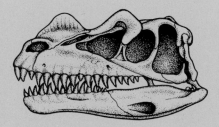

The skull of *Ceratosaurus*, like that of
other carnosaurs, was lightly built and
springy. This enabled the jaws to stretch
to gulp down large chunks of meat. It
was decorated with a horn and brow
ridges, which were unusual features.

# CERATOSAURUS

It is a stormy night on the wind-swept hills above the sprawling marshy plains of Upper Jurassic North America. Disturbed by the rumblings of the thunder in the hills and valleys, two *Ceratosaurus* stumble and slither among the rocky outcrops, their great claws finding it hard to grip on the loose boulders. Lightning splits the darkness of the sky and the two meat-eaters, whose attacks cause terror among the other animal life of the area, wince in a terror of their own. Soon, however, the storm will pass and, in the dawn, the two *Ceratosaurus* will descend to the river plains to seek their prey among the great herbivores there. But the danger of the storm will not be over. The rivers, swelled by the night's torrential rain, may trap the unsuspecting dinosaurs and sweep them to their deaths, entombing them in the beds of sand and shingle that will become the Morrison Formation.

*Ceratosaurus* was one of the smaller and more active of the flesh-eating carnosaurs. The carnosaurs were all the same general shape. They stood on two feet, with the body held forward and balanced over the hips by the long stiff tail; the forelimbs were smaller than the hindlimbs. The animals had a battery of fierce teeth, and the head was carried bird-like, at right angles to the neck. *Ceratosaurus* differed in detail from its relatives. It had a horn on its nose, heavy ridges above the eyes, and a jagged crest down the back. The horn and ridges may have been used in head-banging contests between members of the pack to establish the dominance of the leader. Footprints show *Ceratosaurus* to have been an active hunter, prowling the Upper Jurassic forests in packs, and chasing the plant-eating sauropods across the sandbanks and marshes where they lived. The great claws on the hind limbs, and the smaller ones on the forelimbs, would have been the killing weapons. The teeth were too thin and easily broken to be used in battle. They would have been used for shearing the meat from the body of the dead prey.

| CERATOSAURUS | Length: 6m (19½ft) |
|---|---|
| Fossils: found in the Upper Jurassic Morrison Formation | |
| Locality: Colorado and Wyoming, also East Africa | |
| Order: Saurischia<br>Infraorder: Carnosauria | Suborder: Theropoda<br>Family: Megalosauridae |

# COELURUS

As the sun comes up over the thickets of horsetails on the riverbanks that are destined to become the Morrison Formation, the pterosaurs soar and swoop after the early morning insects, just as they are doing all over the world. Yet there are creatures that prey upon the pterosaurs. A *Coelurus* bursts from the marshy beds and leaps at a pterosaur that swings too low. The pterosaur dodges and flies to safety, while the *Coelurus* checks itself and turns to seek other prey.

Among the drooping fern and cycad fronds, and the thick beds of horsetails that grew by the sluggish streams, there lived a wide variety of reptiles, mammals, insects and, probably, early birds, all of which would have been prey to *Coelurus*. Also present would have been the rotting carcasses of the larger animals which were the main food of the huge carnivores such as *Ceratosaurus*. *Coelurus* would have been able to slip in between their great talons and, jackal-like, make a nimble getaway with whatever morsel it could seize. Eggs may well have been another item of the *Coelurus* diet.

*Coelurus* was a member of the Coelurosauria, comprising primitive and lightly built relatives of the great carnivores of the time. It was very similar in build and appearance to the early archosaurs of some 75 million years before, from which all the dinosaurs were descended. Its long hind legs had three functioning toes and the animal would have carried its body well forward, balancing it with a long, fairly inflexible tail. On its forelimbs *Coelurus* had three fingers, the first of which faced the other two giving a primitive form of thumb. This made the hand a very efficient grasping tool – for a reptile.

The creature was once known as *Ornitholestes* ('bird robber'). Its build, especially the formation of its limbs and hands, suggested that *Coelurus* could leap and pounce after fleeing birds. This is quite possible, but so far no fossils of birds have been found in the Morrison Formation where *Coelurus* comes from, though birds are known to have existed in other parts of the world at earlier times.

| COELURUS | | |
|---|---|---|
| Length: 2m (6½ft) | Weight: 30kg (66lb) | |
| Fossils: found in Upper Jurassic Morrison Formation | | |
| Locality: Wyoming | | |
| Order: Saurischia | Suborder: Theropoda | Family: Coeluridae |

The skeleton of *Coelurus* was similar in layout to that of the large meat-eaters, but it was much more lightly built.

Three possible ways the plates along the
back of *Stegosaurus* could have been arranged.

# STEGOSAURUS

The rain hisses down on the shallow backwater of an Upper Jurassic river in North America. It falls as a dull patter among the surrounding stands of conifer and upon the mat of needle debris covering the soil of the forest. It is a tropical downpour. *Stegosaurus* wades, unheeding, through the shallow water, the rain coursing down its tall flanks, running down its back between its plates and dripping from the end of its nose. Its movements are slow. The chill of the rain is slowly penetrating its great body and making it sluggish. Eventually, however, the downpour passes. The sun dries the vegetation in swirls of steam and forest smells. Warmth seeps back into the great bulk of *Stegosaurus* and it will soon be active enough to seek its food in the lush vegetation of the jungle plain.

*Stegosaurus* is one of the best known dinosaurs. Yet there is still much discussion as to how the animal lived. It was a plant-eater, that much is clear from the teeth and the size of the body. But why did *Stegosaurus* have that incredible array of plates down its back? The plates were only embedded in the skin, they were not attached to the main skeleton. Hence it is not clear how they were arranged on the animal. They probably stuck upright in a double row along the spine, but they may have lain flat along the flanks. If they were in an upright double row, were they arranged in pairs, or alternately? Were they there for defence, to protect the vulnerable backbone from the attacks of the taller carnivores? Or were they a heat regulation device, to increase the surface area of the animal, acting as radiators or extra absorbers of the sun's warmth? Such controversies are typical of the exciting state of modern palaeontology. Every discovery produces something new, and stimulates more arguments.

---

STEGOSAURUS

| | |
|---|---|
| Length: 9m (29ft) | Height at hips: 2.5m (8ft) |
| Fossils: found in the Upper Jurassic Morrison Formation | |
| Locality: Colorado | |
| Order: Ornithischia | Suborder: Stegosauria    Family: Stegosauridae |

# IGUANODON AND HYPSILOPHODON

Along the wooded shore of the Wealden Lake stretching from southern England to France in the Lower Cretaceous period, the placid waters lap quietly against the mudbanks. In the shade, between the trunks of the conifers and cycads, a number of ornithopod dinosaurs move. An individual *Iguanodon* leaves the herd and paddles into the still water to drink. It looks up smartly as a splash sounds, but then returns to its drinking. The splash is made by *Hypsilophodon*, a small relative of *Iguanodon*. *Hypsilophodon* has leapt from the cover of the cycads and is running swiftly across the shallows at the edge of the lake. Both creatures are harmless herbivores, and have nothing to fear from one another.

Until the early 1970s it was thought that *Hypsilophodon* climbed trees. The idea came from a suggestion that the smallest of the four toes on its hind foot pointed backwards and would have been able to grasp the bough of a tree, like perching birds today. However, more detailed study has now shown that this toe did not point backwards, and that the whole leg was well adapted for running. Like its ancestors the thecodonts, *Hypsilophodon* had rows of bony lumps down its back. Most of the other dinosaur groups had lost this feature, including the vast majority of the ornithopods.

*Iguanodon* is one of the best known of all dinosaurs. The discovery of a number of complete skeletons in Belgium in 1878 gave a good idea of *Iguanodon*'s appearance, habits and environment. It is thought a tragedy occurred that resulted in the mass deaths.

| | | |
|---|---|---|
| IGUANODON | Length: 9m (29ft) | |
| Fossils: found in Upper Jurassic Purbeck Beds and Lower Cretaceous Wealden Beds | | |
| Locality: widespread. Most significantly in England and northern Europe, but also in Rumania, Mongolia, north Africa and North America. | | |
| Order: Ornithischia | Suborder: Ornithopoda | Family: Iguanodontidae |
| HYPSILOPHODON | Length: 2m (6½ft) | |
| Fossils: in Lower Cretaceous Wealden marls | Locality: Isle of Wight, England | |
| Order: Ormithischia | Suborder: Ornithopoda | Family: Hypsilophodontidae |

The pointed beak at the front and the grinding teeth
at the back of the skulls of *Iguanodon* (1) and
*Hypsilophodon* (2) tell us these dinosaurs were
plant-eaters.

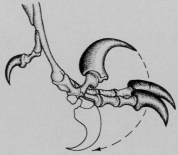

*Deinonychus*, like a number of its relatives, walked on the third and fourth toes only. The first was small but the second carried the huge claw that could be swung through 180° in attack.

# DEINONYCHUS

On a hillside above the moist forested plain that was Montana in the Lower Cretaceous, a *Tenontosaurus* browses, alone and open to attack. The iguanodont has left the safety and cover of the trees and is munching new and different plants on the sunny slopes. This has been a dangerous move, since it has made the animal very noticeable, and liable to be spotted by sharp-eyed predators. Above the rocks further up the slope there stalks a pack of *Deinonychus*. These lightly-built theropod dinosaurs are agile and intelligent. They see the *Tenontosaurus* from afar and immediately spring to the attack, sprinting nimbly down the hillside. As they run, two young males jostle one another; these two have recently been engaged in minor scuffles to assert their dominance within the pack. As the other members of the pack surround the *Tenontosaurus*, they rush to join them. Hissing and spitting, each *Deinonychus* throws itself upon the unfortunate beast, leaping and slashing at its flanks and soft underbelly with vicious sickle-like claws, balancing with their stiff tails and sending swift, well-aimed kicks at their prey. The *Tenontosaurus* eventually staggers and falls. Silence descends, and from a distance, all that can be seen is a group of tawny bodies and waving tails clustered around a mess of blood on the hillside.

The discovery of *Deinonychus* in 1964 provided evidence of a group of dinosaurs that scientists did not know existed. Palaeontologists were coming to the conclusion that the great meat-eaters must have been merely slow-moving scavengers without the ability to mount swift, ferocious attacks. Then remains of *Deinonychus* were unearthed, revealing an animal that was lightly-built, able to run swiftly like an ostrich, and that had a pair of sickle-shaped claws as vicious and deadly as the teeth of a sabre-toothed tiger. What is more, several *Deinonychus* remains were found grouped round a dead *Tenontosaurus*, suggesting a kill made by a hunting pack.

| | |
|---|---|
| DEINONYCHUS | Length: 3m (10ft) |
| Fossils: found in Lower Cretaceous Cloverly Formation | |
| Locality: Montana | |
| Order: Saurischia | Suborder: Theropoda |
| Infraorder: Deinonychosauria | Family: Dromaeosauridae |

# SPINOSAURUS

At a waterhole – one of the many across the river plains of Cretaceous north Africa – a *Spinosaurus* has been lying in the mud. Its fin catches the rays of the early morning sun and spreads the warmth through its body. Before long the smaller animals are up and active. A medium-sized plant-eating dinosaur lopes down to the water's edge to drink, unaware of danger. *Spinosaurus* does not have the wit to remain in hiding and to plan an ambush. It heaves itself out of the mud as soon as it sees this likely looking meal and attacks. The herbivore, paralysed with fear, hesitates a moment too long and the straight, shearing teeth of *Spinosaurus* close on its neck, ripping through bone and soft tissue. The doomed animal flops into the mud and writhes for a time, the hind feet jerking and the tail threshing – and then it is still. Large scavenging storks that had been soaring above on the lookout for a kill, come planing down and settle around to wait for *Spinosaurus* to finish feeding.

Several of the larger dinosaurs living in open areas had fins on their backs. These fins were supported by strong spines that projected upwards from the vertebrae. In this way they resembled the fins of the pelycosaurs of the Permian period. They probably served the very same function – as a heat control mechanism. With the panel of skin and blood vessels held at right angles to the early morning sun, the blood could be warmed more quickly than if the sun's warmth had to penetrate the whole body. Later, when the sun was at its hottest, the creature could sit in whatever shade was available and hold the fin to catch the wind, thus carrying away the excess heat.

*Spinosaurus* was the largest known of these fin-backed dinosaurs. The spines themselves were about 1.8 metres (6 feet) long, making a very impressive fin on the back of an animal that otherwise resembled *Tyrannosaurus* in size and shape. It may be that the fin served another purpose, as a display signal that enabled animals of the same species to recognize one another or that warned enemies to keep away.

| SPINOSAURUS | Length: 12m (39ft) |
|---|---|
| Fossils: found in the Upper Cretaceous Bahairia Formation | |
| Locality: Egypt and Niger | |
| Order: Saurischia<br>Infraorder: Carnosauria | Suborder: Theropoda<br>Family: Spinosauridae |

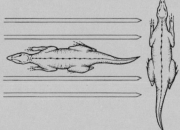

When a fin-backed dinosaur turned at right-angles to the sun, the fin absorbed the sun's heat. When the animal was facing into the sun the fin radiated heat away.

Pterosaur wingspans varied from the
enormous 12 metres of *Quetzalcoatlus*
(1) to 25 centimetres for *Pterodactylus*
(3) *Pteranodon* (2) was 7 metres.

# QUETZALCOATLUS

The late afternoon sun floods the plains of Upper Cretaceous North America and falls on the body of an old *Triceratops* that has just collapsed and died. Several kilometres away, in the sky, a number of black shapes are circling. A flock of *Quetzalcoatlus*, the largest flying creatures ever to have lived, are soaring in a column of warm air. With keen eyesight one of the great creatures notices the distant form of the *Triceratops* and, with a harsh squawk, it angles its wings and turns out of the thermal to begin its long glide towards this likely looking meal. The others of the group instantly notice its descent and follow it. Soon the ground on which the body lies is darkened by the shadows of great wings gliding down from above. One *Quetzalcoatlus* lands, and pecks at an eye. Another stabs at the soft skin of the belly. In a few minutes the corpse is covered with a squabbling mass of jabbing beaks and flapping wings and the rib-cage is exposed.

*Quetzalcoatlus* was the largest pterosaur known, and in size must have been as big as it is possible for any airborne animal to be. Its bones, found in Texas in 1971, show that the creature had a wingspan of about 12 metres (39 feet). Up to this time the biggest pterosaur to be discovered was *Pteranodon*, with a wingspan of 7 metres (23 feet). *Pteranodon* probably lived on seaside cliffs and swooped for fishes in the sea. *Quetzalcoatlus*, however, lived a great distance away from the sea on open flat land. It must have been a scavenger, just like today's vultures. Like the other pterosaurs *Quetzalcoatlus* was covered with hair – necessary for the fine control of temperature needed for a life of flight. However, like vultures, its head and neck were probably naked. Hair would have become fouled with blood as the creatures pecked around inside body cavities and rib-cages.

The pterosaurs were subdivided into two suborders. The Rhamphorynchoidea were the more primitive and existed until Upper Jurassic times. The Pterodactyloidea, to which *Quetzalcoatlus* belonged, lived until the end of the reptiles' heyday.

| QUETZALCOATLUS | Wingspan: 12m (39ft) |
|---|---|
| Fossils: found in Upper Cretaceous terrestrial siltstones and sandstones | |
| Locality: Big Bend National Park, Texas | |
| Order: Pterosauria | Suborder: Pterodactyloidea |

# STRUTHIOMIMUS

It is a damp and misty early morning. A group of *Struthiomimus* are out foraging. They move slowly about, pecking at plants with their toothless beaks, snapping up insects or small lizards, and perhaps plundering the nests of other dinosaurs. And all the while they also keep a lookout for danger. When two of them have their heads down, the third is head up, alert. Suddenly, across the shrubby vegetation, one detects a movement that could be an approaching predator. With a hiss of warning it springs off, the others instantly following. Splashing through the puddles they speed away from danger at some 80 kilometres (50 miles) an hour.

The 'ostrich dinosaurs', of which *Struthiomimus* was a typical example, were the last of the coelurosaurs. They evolved during the Lower Cretaceous and existed through to the end of that period. They are well named; their hind legs were long and thin, built for speed, and their light skulls were carried bird-like at right-angles to their slender necks.
. Some members of the group had very large eyes, suitable for night prowling. Their forelegs were also quite long, but not as long as the hind, and were equipped with three-fingered grasping hands. The body was normally held horizontally, balanced by a long rigid tail. The 'ostrich dinosaurs' probably ate small reptiles and mammals and may also have raided the nests of larger beasts.

| STRUTHIOMIMUS | | |
| --- | --- | --- |
| Length: 4m (13ft) | Height: 2m (6½ft) | |
| Fossils: found in the Upper Cretaceous Oldman and Edmonton Formations | | |
| Locality: Alberta | | |
| Order: Saurischia | Suborder: Theropoda | Family: Ornithomimidae |

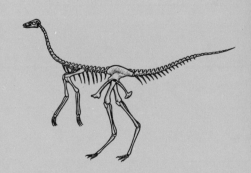

The outward similarity between *Struthiomimus* and the large flightless birds of today shows that they probably lived in a similar environment (see page 16).

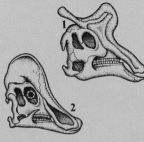

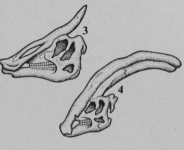

Duck-billed dinosaur crests developed from the bones of the nose. Most were hollow and contained nasal passages to enhance the sense of smell, and to amplify the animals' bellowing. Those shown here are *Lambeosaurus* (1), *Corythosaurus* (2), *Saurolophus* (3) and *Parasaurolophus* (4).

# LAMBEOSAURUS

In a sunny glade of the Upper Cretaceous forest, in the foothills of North America, magnolia bushes are in full bloom, catching the sunlight that reaches them through a gap in the surrounding woodland of oak, ash, birch and willow. The landscape could be of a present-day forest. But the animal life is quite different. There is a rustle and a squawk in the branches, and a small flurry of pterosaurs are startled from their rest, flapping off across the clearing at the approach of something large. The large animal turns out to be a *Lambeosaurus*, one of the crested duck-billed dinosaurs, wandering through the trees on its own. It stops in the sunlight and, with its long tongue, picks a bunch of twigs and chews them up. Grinding up the leaves and blossoms with its many tightly packed teeth, it circulates the pulp round its cheek-pouches before swallowing. Then, it raises its head, utters a loud trumpeting call to keep in touch with the rest of the herd, and lumbers on through the forest.

In form, the duck-billed dinosaurs resembled *Iguanodon*, but their skulls showed a development of a duck-like beak and a massive array of grinding teeth. Their strong hind legs had three toes tipped with hoofs. The smaller front legs had four toes, two of which had hoofs. The animals were probably bipedal, but could go on all fours as well. There were webs of skin between the fingers, and the tail was flattened from side to side. This may indicate that they spent at least part of their time in the water. Many, including *Lambeosaurus*, had strange and extravagant crests protruding from their skulls.

The duck-billed dinosaurs ranged over the whole of the northern hemisphere and their remains have also been found in South America. In 1979 a number of nests of *Maiasaura* were discovered in Montana. Consisting of mounds of mud, they contained a number of young in quite an advanced stage of development. This indicates that the adults looked after the young for some time after hatching.

| LAMBEOSAURUS | Length: 7m (23ft) |
|---|---|
| Fossils: found in the Upper Cretaceous Oldman Formation | |
| Locality: Red Deer River, Alberta, Canada | |
| Order: Ornithischia<br>Family: Hadrosauridae | Suborder: Ornithopoda<br>Subfamily: Lambeosaurinae |

# PALAEOSCINCUS

Along the Upper Cretaceous riverbank the clouds of insects swarm and dance in the early afternoon sun. Through the waterside vegetation the great bulk of a *Palaeoscincus* moves, slowly, heavily. The insects are all around it, gathering in its eyes and nostrils, and settling on its armour-plated back. *Palaeoscincus* ignores them. In fact it hardly notices them, since its nervous system is not fine enough to react to such minor irritations. It browses among the shrubs regardless. However, a small flock of egret-like birds do notice, and they follow the beast as it waddles along. They settle upon its back and fly down to the ground to chase and snap up the small creatures disturbed by the plodding of the great feet. *Palaeoscincus* hardly notices the birds either. It would take a very large animal to attract its attention.

*P*alaeoscincus was one of the first dinosaurs to be discovered in the United States. This was in the 1850s, and only the teeth were found. A partial skeleton was discovered later which showed it to be one of the heavily armoured ankylosaurs.

The Ankylosauria were one of the four suborders of the Ornithischia. They were all fairly squat, tank-like animals, equipped with heavy armour over the back. In some this armour consisted of scattered bony plates. In others it was like a fine mosaic. Some, like *Palaeoscincus*, had spikes projecting from the side. Others had spikes sticking up from the back. With this armour the ankylosaurs were perfectly protected on their upper surfaces. With the development of the armour some of the later larger examples, such as *Palaeoscincus*, became broad and sprawling. They were unprotected on the underside, but it would have been unlikely that any flesh-eating dinosaur, however big, could have turned them over and attacked them in the belly. The ankylosaurs were very numerous and successful. They may have been the most abundant dinosaurs on the North American landscape at the end of the Cretaceous period.

| PALAEOSCINCUS | Length: 5m (16ft) | |
|---|---|---|
| Fossils: in the Upper Cretaceous Judith River and Two Medicine Formations | | |
| Locality: Montana | | |
| Order: Ornithischia | Suborder: Ankylosauria | Family: Nodosauridae |

The ankylosaurs showed a great
variation in armour. Some had plates
and spikes on the back, others had a
knob on the tail. Shown here are
*Silvisaurus* (1) and
*Scolosaurus* (2).

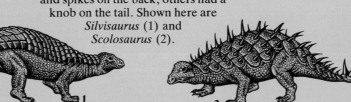

# TYRANNOSAURUS

A still, blue soda lake shimmers beneath the sun in Upper Cretaceous North America. Its mineral-rich waters are a soup of blue-green algae and water fleas. Thousands of flamingo-like birds wade along the shore, feeding on the microscopic plants and tiny creatures in the shallow water. Along the upper shore, boiling springs bubble up, with clouds of steam visible even in the midday heat. Where the fresher water from these springs flows down to the lake, the birds gather to drink. Beside a boiling spring waddles a *Tyrannosaurus*, one of the largest of the flesh-eating dinosaurs; the birds fly past the huge animal as if it were a rocky outcrop. But there is nothing here for a *Tyrannosaurus* to eat; it feeds on carrion.

*Tyrannosaurus* has always been thought of as the most ferocious of the dinosaurs. In fact, it probably was not very fierce at all. The leg joints and the position of the feet show that it could take only very short steps – less than a metre – and that it could move only at about 5 kilometres (3 miles) per hour. It could hardly have chased and fought with the other animals of the time. Its 15 centimetre (6 inch) long teeth were saw-edged and ideal for slicing up meat. However, they were very thin and would have been easily broken in any kind of a fight. All this suggests that *Tyrannosaurus* was a scavenger, eating only the bodies of animals that had already died or had been killed by more active predators. Once it had found the body of a large plant-eating dinosaur, *Tyrannosaurus* could squat down by it and strip off the meat until its belly was full. After a long siesta it would rise to its feet, using its tiny two-fingered forelimbs to steady itself on the way up, and wander off in search of its next meal.

| TYRANNOSAURUS | Length: 12m (39ft) |
|---|---|
| Fossils: found in Upper Cretaceous Hell Creek Formation | |
| Locality: Montana and possibly in China | |
| Order: Saurischia<br>Infraorder: Carnosauria | Suborder: Theropoda<br>Family: Tyrannosauridae |

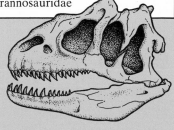

The skull of *Tyrannosaurus*, like that of other carnosaurs, was loosely jointed, so that it could dislocate its jaws like a snake and gulp down great chunks of meat.

# PACHYCEPHALOSAURUS

The wooded mountainside echoes to a loud 'Thwack!' Birdsong among the conifers ceases. The sound comes again. 'Thwack!' And again. 'Thwack!' Two male *Pachycephalosaurus* are sparring for territory. Much of the action is bluff and display. At a distance from one another the two animals rear up as tall as they can, shaking their heavy heads and nodding slowly, up and down, up and down, presenting to each other the bright warning colours on their heads and chests. Then they charge. Their heads come down, their tails go up, and they tilt into one another. 'Thwack!' The impact is taken on the massive bony head-dome and sends shudders down through the horizontal neck and back. Then they immediately rear up for another session of nodding display. Meanwhile, the drab females stand further down the slope, browsing, unconcerned with the drama that is taking place about their future. Soon the weaker of the two males tires. It backs away, turns and goes off up the slope. It will live alone for now, but some day it will be stronger. Then it will put up a real fight for ownership of the territory and the females that live in it.

The pachycephalosaurs, or 'bone-heads', developed in the Lower Cretaceous but reached their peak in Upper Cretaceous times. They evolved from the same stock as the iguanodonts, and were like them in many ways; they stood on two feet and were herbivorous. Their most remarkable feature was the dome-like development of the skull. Made of solid bone, this could withstand great impact and pressures from the top. It was obviously used in combat, as a battering ram. However, such a structure could not have done much serious damage and so it is thought that it was used in tests of strength, to decide which male should lead the herd. Most of the pachycephalosaurs were quite small – about 2 metres (6½ feet) in length.

Most pachycephalosaur remains, found in river deposits, consist of merely the bony head lump, worn smooth by water. It is thought that these animals lived in the highlands and only rarely were their bodies also washed downstream and fossilized.

| PACHYCEPHALOSAURUS | Length: 5m (16ft) |
|---|---|
| Fossils: found in Upper Cretaceous Lance Formation | |
| Locality: Montana, Wyoming and South Dakota | |
| Order: Ornithischia | Suborder: Ornithopoda |
| Family: Pachycephalosauridae | |

The bony dome of *Pachycephalosaurus* was 25 centimetres thick. It also had spikes on its nose and around the back of its skull. Its neck vertebrae were stiffened and strengthened to help withstand impacts.

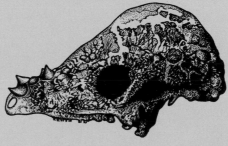

The heavy armour of a *Triceratops* skull means that, unlike other dinosaurs, fossils of the skull have often been found. More than fifteen species of *Triceratops* have been described, with different sizes and shapes of horns. Shown here are *T. brevicornis* (1), *T. elatus* (2), *T. serratus* (3) and *T. albertiensis* (4).

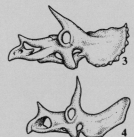

# TRICERATOPS

A bright chill autumn morning finds a solitary *Triceratops* exposed in a clearing, its breath hanging mistily on the still, cold air. Normally it can rely on its bulk to contain enough warmth from the previous day to see it through the nights that are becoming colder. But now the days themselves are cool, and the animal is becoming more and more sluggish as the Age of Dinosaurs draws to a close.

*Triceratops* was the largest and most spectacular, as well as one of the last, of the ceratopsians. It carried three particularly long horns on its head. A solid bone shield swept backwards over its shoulders. These alarming features must have been used in ritual display between *Triceratops* individuals as well as defence against predators. The rear legs were straight and pillar-like, providing a firm support. The shorter forelegs were more manoeuvrable, so that the animal could turn and swing its shoulders and head round to face threat from any direction. Display for dominance between males would have ended with a powerful shoving match as the combatants locked their heads together and pushed and butted until the weaker gave way. Damage to fossil head shields shows evidence of this.

The ceratopsians were purely plant-eaters. Their hooked beaks were suitable for nipping off shoots. The back teeth worked like a pair of scissors, chopping up leaves and vegetable matter that could be churned around in the cheek pouches. When the climate changed in the northern continents, however, the vegetation also changed. Subtropical forest was replaced by stands of conifers, making it difficult for the dinosaurs to find enough food. *Triceratops*, one of the most successful of the dinosaurs, was headed for extinction.

| | |
|---|---|
| TRICERATOPS | Length: up to 11m (36ft) |
| Length of skull: 2m (6½ft) | Weight: 8.5 tonnes |
| Fossils: found in Upper Cretaceous Lance Formation | |
| Locality: Wyoming, Colorado, Montana, Saskatchewan | |
| Order: Ornithischia Suborder: Ceratopsia Family: Ceratopsidae | |

# GLOSSARY

**Ammonite** Extinct cephalod that resembled an octopus in a coiled shell.

**Amphibian** Member of the class of animals which evolved as a form in between the fish and reptiles. Amphibians lay eggs in the water but the adult lives on land. Frogs and newts are amphibians.

**Ankylosaurs** Group of ornithischian dinosaurs protected by bony armour and spikes over the back and tail; e.g. *Palaeoscincus*.

**Archosaurs** The ruling reptile group to which the dinosaurs and pterosaurs belonged. Crocodiles are archosaurs.

**Bipedal** Walking on two legs.

**Carnosaurs** Group of large theropod saurischian dinosaurs; e.g. *Tyrannosaurus*.

**Cephalopod** Member of the class of invertebrate animals with tentacles attached to their heads. Squids and octopus are cephalopods.

**Ceratopsians** Group of ornithischian dinosaurs with armoured heads and horns; e.g. *Triceratops*.

**Coelurosaurs** Group of small theropod saurischian dinosaurs; e.g. *Coelurus, Saltopus*.

**Cold-blooded** A misleading term given to those vertebrates that cannot regulate their body temperatures, as can mammals and birds.

**Dicynodonts** Group of mammal-like reptiles with a pair of dog-like teeth; e.g. *Lystrosaurus*.

**Hadrosaurs** Group of ornithopod ornithischian dinosaurs with duck-like skulls and, sometimes, extravagant crests; e.g. *Lambeosaurus*.

**Ichthyosaurs** Group of fish-shaped swimming reptiles; e.g. *Ophthalmosaurus*.

**Invertebrate** An animal with no backbone. This term covers the whole animal kingdom except for the fishes, amphibians, reptiles, mammals and birds.

**Mammal** Member of the most advanced vertebrate group in terms of evolution. Mammals bear their young alive and suckle them and usually have hair. Cats, whales, horses and human beings are mammals.

**Metabolic rate** The relative speed at which the chemical and physical processes take place inside a living body. Cold-blooded animals have a low metabolic rate, while warm-blooded animals have a high metabolic rate.

**Nothosaurs** Group of aquatic reptiles which were probably ancestors to the plesiosaurs; e.g. *Nothosaurus*.

**Ornithischians** Subgroup of the archosaurs with pelvis like that of a bird, hence bird-hipped.

**Ornithopods** Group of ornithischian dinosaurs which were bipedal and had feet similar to those of birds; e.g. *Iguanodon, Lambeosaurus, Pachycephalosaurus*.

**Pachycephalosaurs** Group of ornithopod ornithischian dinosaurs with thick bony skulls; e.g. *Pachycephalosaurus*.

**Pelycosaurs** The earliest development in the line of mammal-like reptiles. They were lizard-like and most had a sail on the back; e.g. *Dimetrodon*.

**Plesiosaurs** Group of swimming reptiles with a turtle-like body and limbs and a long neck or long head; e.g. *Cryptocleidus, Macroplata*.

**Pliosaurs** Group of long-headed plesiosaurs; e.g. *Macroplata*.

**Procompsognathids** The most primitive subdivision of the coelurosaur group; e.g. *Saltopus*.

**Prosauropods** Group of long-necked saurischian dinosaurs that could be bipedal or go on all fours. Their diet comprised either plants or animals and they may have been ancestors of the sauropods; e.g. *Thecodontosaurus*.

**Pterosaurs** Group of flying and gliding archosaurs; e.g. *Pterodactylus*.

**Reptile** Member of the class of animals that lays eggs on land. Reptiles are scaly. Lizards, snakes and crocodiles belong to this class.

**Rhynchosaurs** A primitive lizard-like group of reptiles related to today's tuatara of New Zealand; e.g. *Hyperodapedon*.

**Saurischians** Subgroup of the archosaurs with pelvis like that of a normal reptile, hence lizard-hipped.

**Sauropods** Group of heavy long-necked saurischian dinosaurs; e.g. *Diplodocus*.

**Theropods** Group of meat-eating saurischian dinosaurs; e.g. *Tyrannosaurus, Coelurus, Saltopus*.

**Vertebrate** An animal with a backbone. All fish, amphibians, reptiles, mammals and birds are vertebrates.

**Warm-blooded** A misleading term given to those vertebrates that have a high metabolic rate and can control their own body temperatures.

# INDEX

# HOUSE ACKNOWLEDGEMENTS

### Editorial and design

| | |
|---|---|
| Editorial Director | Ian Jackson |
| Art Editor | Nigel Partridge |
| Copy Editor | Geraldine Christy |
| Proof Reader | Jocelyn Selson |
| Indexer | Jackie Pinhey |
| Production | Bob Towell |

### Photographs

Some of the photographs incorporate background photography by Norman Tomalin, Paul Wakefield, David Houston and Jan Taylor.

The photograph on page 6 is by Jane Burton.

### Drawings

The drawing on page 20 (centre) is reproduced by permission of the British Museum (Natural History).

### Artists

All artwork of reptiles featured in the photographs by Steve Kirk.

Colour artwork within the introduction by Alan Male, with the exception of pages 24–25 by Richard Hook, both represented by Linden Artists Ltd.

Line drawings by Paul Robinson, represented by Artist Partners, with the exception of page 20 (top) by Andrew Farmer.

Retouching by Kay Robinson, with the exception of the photograph on page 52 by Brian Bull.

Eddison/Sadd Editions acknowledges with grateful thanks the assistance received from the staff of the palaeontology library of the British Museum (Natural History).